A Lizard, a Parakeet,
and a
Methodist
Grandmother

A Lizard, a Parakeet,
and a
Methodist
Grandmother

—⚬⚬⚬—

Michael Broome

— for Em and Jo, whose love and support
and gracious good humor over the years
have enhanced my life
— best wishes always—

Michael Broome

Charleston, SC
www.PalmettoPublishing.com

A Lizard, a Parakeet, and a Methodist Grandmother

First Edition

Paperback ISBN: 978-1-63837-653-8
eBook ISBN: 978-1-63837-654-5

This book is memoir. It reflects the author's present
recollecions of experiences over time. Some names and
characteristics have been changed, some events have been
compressed, and some dialogue has been recreated.

Dedication

—for my sons, Steve and Paul, and their families, who seem to enjoy my ramblings and who, on occasion, even laugh

—for my Alabama family, Pat and Jim, and for my South Carolina family—Carol, Billy, Suzanne, and Randy—who know the stories

—for my chosen families: my amigos, Deborah, Rick, and Sam, whose Southern roots parallel mine and whose friendship I treasure; my former neighbors and fellow cat lovers, Carolyn and David, whose closeness and support never change through the years; and my "Post Oak" sister and brother, Pat and Roy, who've known us and loved us for a long time

—and for my dear wife, Charlotte, whose advice, counsel, and love always inform my happiness

Table of Contents

Introduction

Please read this "Introduction." Some of what I'm trying to do in these stories might make more sense if you start off here.

It's necessary that you understand the setting for my remembrances. Post Oak, Georgia, was a small town with a population of some 1,500 when I was growing up there in the 1950s. Chattanooga, Tennessee, was eighteen miles to the north and fulfilled its role as our nearby "big city" with large department stores, movie theaters, nice restaurants, and limited sports venues. Post Oak was Landsford County's county seat and served as a point of supply for the area's farms, still a mail drop and agricultural products offloading facility by means of a railroad line, and a growing town with three drug stores; three small-town grocery stores; two five- and ten-cent stores; two hardware stores; four gas stations; five churches; two barber shops; three beauty shops; a good-sized bank; two doctors' offices; a Masonic lodge; a volunteer fire department with two used fire trucks; a town police department with a 1956 Plymouth police car and two full-time police officers; the county sheriff's office with the sheriff, six full-time deputies, and four modified Ford cruisers replete with souped-up 312 cu. in. V8s. (Into the mid-1960s these Fords morphed into six 389 cu. in. Pontiac GTOs that paid for themselves by means of effective fee grabbing on Donkey Patch Road and I-75.);

a recently rebuilt grammar school; an upgraded junior high school; a new high school with a roof and plumbing service that did not accord with state construction standards; and an even lesser quality grammar school for the town's black students. Convoys of school busses left school parking areas daily for the county's outlying sections, mostly farms and modest residential communities. The rest, the town kids, were lined up at each school's front doors and dispatched with teachers' warnings not to misbehave during the walks home. The grammar school proudly sported four "school patrol" officers wearing white shoulder straps and badges. Each officer monitored his route with a watchful eye, a small notebook to record those who dared to depart from the rules, and an eager stride toward substantive intersections to stop cars for student protection at these crossings. I was one of these patrol officers for two years and could boast of sending six offenders to the principal's office for spankings. For most of my childhood, our telephones were reached by four-digit phone numbers. One garbage collector, Mr. McDowell, picked up our trash once each week in his aging dump truck (To replace him one day was my chief career aspiration.). Three traffic lights regulated the moderate flow of cars and semis through Post Oak.

These stories will tempt me to triteness. But in all truth, our community's citizens typically didn't lock doors at night, looked out for each other in times of family distress, tried to support local businesses whenever possible, were eager to attend their children's school plays and sports events, and could, literally, keep an eye on each others' kids who might not always go home to dinner at the appointed times. The phone hotline would kick into high parent notification if one of us got into trouble, back talked an authority figure, or was seen messing around building sites, the abandoned cannery, or wrecked cars behind Mr. Marshman's body shop. We were able to play army all day without reporting in to parents or grandparents, but we also knew that, with all due respect to George Orwell, "big brother was watching." I hope many readers will be able to relate to my descriptions here and recall with fondness and nostalgia. These were good times in a good place.

These stories will probably interest no one but me. That's OK, though. I'm a retired college English teacher who once relished the design and teaching of a course in Southern Literature taken primarily by English majors. It used to help, I thought, that I was a Southerner from a small northwest Georgia town, educated in the South, and so much fascinated by the writings of Southerners who had made it. I still believe that a bonafide Southern boy (or girl) possesses something ingrained, something cultural, maybe, that enables him (or her) to know the South better than those "from off," as one of my Pawley's Island, South Carolina, friends would say. I hope I'm right.

It used to matter to me that my students could identify the form or identifying traits of a specific piece of literature. "You will get more out of this," I would say at the beginning of the term, "and you can win Jeopardy games on the large screen TV at your local watering hole if you know the rhyme scheme of an Italian sonnet or the characteristics of a mock epic or the narrative mode called 'stream of consciousness' or the handling of plot in an episodic novel or iambic pentameter or a tragic flaw. These things will be on your tests, of course." And I once honestly believed that this knowledge made you a better student of literature. Now I'm not so sure. Maybe it's better just to be a close reader and to have an openness about what you're reading . . . and to accept the invitation to someone else's life-view and experiences.

What I've tried to do is to write about some people and some events and some other things that were important to me. I've also tried to include local color details about what mattered to a small boy when he was nine or ten and collected baseball cards, played with his Lionel train, fished at the creek with his buddies, rode his bicycle around the court house, shot his Daisy BB pump gun at Coke bottles and once at a bird, visited an alligator farm in Florida, vacationed at the Moon-Glo Motel in Panama City, watched a bunch of grown men try to extricate a stuck tractor trailer from a town underpass, and gave his sleeping dad an unwanted haircut. "The devil is in the details," I've always heard. Here I hope that these details, as I remember them, will not become the devil's work but will, instead, add a bit of life and memory to these ramblings.

If these writings make it to some form of publication, I'll no doubt be asked whether these things all actually happened. And I won't quite know how to answer. Certainly, names and places have been altered. After all, law suits can be messy things. I've found out as I listed several events worth the re-telling that the memory is indeed a curious phenomenon. What I could have sworn was the gospel in my recollections often has been negated during conversations with my high school classmates during reunions or during vacations spent with special friends and family. Or maybe these other folks are the ones who don't have it right. Whatever the case, it's worth the time to sit down and write events of your past. If you do, you'll appreciate these moments even more. Faulkner said one time, "The past isn't dead. It isn't even past." I reckon, if you could chop us Southerners open without causing a grisly, fatal mishmash, you'd find a substantial piece of each of us labeled "past," maybe located a few inches above the heart and almost overlapping the soul. And for us, this piece goes a long way toward making us what and who we are.

So I would answer that, yes, these events really happened, and each was the basis of something important in my life. But in most cases—not all, but most—some of the people and actions and locations were squeezed or distilled or refined to make a more complete reflection. In all of this overhauling of experience, I suppose I caved to some god or goddess of literature—to make something that was quite episodic and piecemeal become more coherent. But, dammit, if a famous sculptor can change the gender of the Muses at Brookgreen Gardens, South Carolina, then I can take certain liberties with that "past" piece inside me. Can't I?

One of my recent favorite Southern writers—maybe it was Pat Conroy or Rick Bragg or Roy Blount or someone else—said one time that "the truth shouldn't get in the way of a good story." I hope that some of these stories are at least passable and that I haven't played loose with the truth too much. Thanks for reading.

Michael Broome
May 2021

The Christening Gown

The sacrament of baptism—or christening, as the rite is called in most Wesleyan circles—didn't have many takers in 1948 in the First Methodist Church of Post Oak, Georgia. When it did take place, it usually attracted a crowd, especially in my family. This serene, blessed ritual, when it was my turn, was reported to have caused major upheaval in my family and a series of events that challenged the propriety and grace of my deeply devout grandmother.

From time immemorial, my family has been Methodist. My grandmother, Franny Millwood, was always the flag bearer of this protestant allegiance, she of the anti-Baptist, anti-Presbyterian, anti-Church of Christ persuasion. She affirmed that these other denominations were only loosely Christian and not nearly as close to the right relationship with God as her beloved Methodist Church. And for her, it followed that all Methodist principles and processes were, in and of themselves, proper and good, especially this approach to baptism. Her pontification on these Methodist rites could become overbearing at times. Granny lived with us until her death when I was ten, and no church event, especially involving our family, could occur without her careful analysis. It's so ironic that my christening, the much anticipated consecration of my little soul to Christ as well as my formal naming, gave rise to a far less-than-sacred family memory.

It must be understood that we Methodists place much stock in the christening version of this sacrament. The chosen candidate may be adult or child or infant. In the case of a baby, the usual candidate, the minister often carefully takes the child from the parents at the altar and briefly faces the congregation so that all assembled are able to see the beautiful little pre-angel.

If you're disturbed enough, as I am, to enjoy amusing departures from expected formal ceremonies, then, with a christening, you can predict this departure at about the same time that the minister turns to the flock. Should the baby begin to squirm and flail the arms and wail and reach out for the parents, then this entire sacramental event will be tainted. The minister can do little to regain control. Most ministers know this and resign themselves to cutting losses and finishing up quickly. After all, the length of the rite has nothing to do with whether or not the christening "takes." And at this point of the baby's maximum squirm, the minister will usually signal the organist with a slight head shake that there will be no ceremonial walk up and down the aisle to show off the recently consecrated infant to the lilting strains of *Jesus Loves Me, This I Know*. But I overtake myself.

The key moment of the sacrament comes when the minister dips her or his hand into the baptismal font, flicks away all but the necessary amount of water, and lightly sprinkles the infant's forehead. This procedure is usually easy. However, it's possible that a family or individual might decide to have a more Baptist-like immersion experience to mark full acceptance of and commitment to Christ. The initiate is fully dunked. Or the initiate can go through a baptism involving the pouring of water over the head. Honestly, I've never seen a Methodist dunking or pouring, but either is allowable. Methodists are indeed open to any of these options.

Bottom line, though, most followers of Wesley prefer what we consider to be the slightly formal, less holy rollerish, light sprinkling certainly more than the messy dunking of the initiate in a large pool of water with its attendant thrashing around, shaking, spluttering, coughing, gasping, even the post-dunk shouting and crying with arms raised in the "I'm a-comin' to you, sweet Jesus" posture. All told, I suppose this baptismal pool idea is less showy than the experience—and I've seen old photos of it—of a large group of white-robed Baptist participants gathered at the local muddy creek for what must be a full River Jordan-inspired immersion. But I'm just twisted enough to think of these photos as resembling a KKK trip to the closest Wally's Water World amusement park. Lord forgive me.

This Sunday of my christening was to be an important day. And everything surrounding it had to be properly ordered and arranged. Not to do so would have been to invite the full wrath of Franny Millwood, my grandmother; Francine Lockhart, my mom; and assorted aunts, uncles, great aunts, great uncles, and layers of cousins from as far away as Savannah.

Mom and Granny had begun preparing for the christening at least four months in advance. First, the preacher himself must be reserved on a date he finds agreeable. The christening gown must be selected. The appropriate family members and friends must be invited. Decisions about the post-christening Sunday dinner must be made: the time, the location (home or a local restaurant), the appropriate people to include. My grandmother and my mom were good about this sort of planning. But all of the meticulous advance planning in the world couldn't forestall the surprising hilarity of my own blessed event. As we continue, I'll try to avoid sacrilege.

Mom coordinated carefully with our preacher, Reverend Morris, a stern, formal, white-bearded, old-fashioned kind of clergyman. To me, in old Kodak photos of the sacred day, he resembled the Old Testament prophet Isaiah, or at least he looked sort of like the paper cut-out of Isaiah that Mrs. Bender, our Sunday School teacher, used to stick up on the painted flannel background boards of a manger, desert oasis with palm trees, temple, or river scene. Nearing retirement in 1948, Reverend Morris was never more in his element than when he could preside at a wedding, funeral, christening, or, even more routinely, communion. As he neared career end, Reverend Morris would still do all right with the ceremony. He wasn't to be the problem.

With the date settled, the co-matriarchs set about the task of selecting just the right christening gown for me. This was something you did in the Post Oak Methodist Church con-gregation in the 1940's. The process was never an issue for Granny. She hinted and hinted and reminisced and reminisced about the christening gown that had belonged to her first-born son and beloved little W. T. This christening gown—at the time of its original use a beautiful, milky white, fragile, cottony, lacey piece—had taken months to sew by hand.

Little W. T. Millwood had died in the flu epidemic in 1918 at age five, and my heretofore solid-as-a-rock grandmother had never quite recovered from this loss. This thirty-year-old passing was only yesterday to Granny. She never tired of telling W. T. stories, those from the little guy's impish side but always balancing them with something with a more angelic twist. He must have been quite a precocious, prank playing, intelligent chap and the object of worship by his mother and father.

Granny's eyes would sparkle—then well up with tears—when she recounted the day he came home with his dad from the barber shop. My granddad would routinely take little W. T. to the barber shop on Saturdays, where Mr. Millwood worked part time to help out ol' Toby Gordy, the town's octogenarian, cantankerous barber. My grandmother cringed at the thought of her precious angel being exposed to the stories, jokes, foul language, tobacco chewing and spitting, and cigar smoking emanating from that horrid cesspool, but she couldn't stop her little boy's exposure. One day, as W. T. and his father returned from town and walked into the kitchen, Granny began her usual tirade: "Lockie (her nickname for granddad), did my angel hear a lot of that plumb awful stuff y'all carry on with in that sinful barber shop? Did he? You tell me now. I've begged you and begged you not to take him there. You don't listen. He picks up those nasty words and says them to everbody. It's plain awful." She reached out to pull W. T. to her side. He slightly resisted this time and began the objection of a five-year-old who relished these trips with his father and wanted nothing to interfere.

"Naw, Murr (his name for his mom), nothin' bad happened. Why, I ain't said *shit* nor nothin' all day." This re-telling always resulted in much family laughter. And on cue, Granny would end the story with W. T.'s childlike vulgarity, without reference to the punishment doled out to Lockie or W. T. You could tell that Granny enjoyed telling this story, but there was a hint of holdover embarrassment, even after the long passage of time.

She would usually mitigate the unintended foul language episode with the story of W. T.'s willing help with breakfast preparation. Always rising early, Franny would move to the kitchen to fix breakfast for Lockie, W. T., and Rebecca, the eldest daughter who came along two years after W. T.'s appearance. The only other family member in the kitchen that early was W. T., barefooted but with his overalls firmly buttoned and with one of the kitchen chairs moved up next to Granny's workplace at the counter. After Granny had rolled out the biscuit dough, W. T. would press the snuff can cutter template onto the dough and produce at least eight biscuits before Granny re-compressed the remaining dough. W. T. never tired of this important role. When this preparation was over, he climbed down from the chair, hugged Granny's leg, told her he loved her, dodged her effort at a quick kiss, and walked with a cocky stride out into the back yard. We all need to be felt necessary at times, I reckon.

As my christening day approached, the important role W. T.'s gown would play never occurred to a single soul. Of course, Mom didn't take Granny's bait regarding W. T.'s gown. My mother was required to fawn over the now faded gown several times a year, each time, in fact, that Granny pulled it out of the old cedar chest to unfold and to pat and to cherish. This regular pulling out and caressing and patting and holding close to a make-up laden face and then the re-folding and re-stuffing amidst old quilts and bedspreads had not contributed to the gown's original pristine appearance. By 1948, this gown was yellowed and stained and sadly wrinkled, and Mom could tell that this relic would be inappropriate for her son's christening before a full sanctuary. How to convince her long-grieving mother to let go of the W. T. gown idea was the issue.

As she ruminated over the handling of Granny, my mother decided to buck tradition regarding family-used, hand-sewn gowns. She would *buy* my christening gown and would insist that Granny come with her to nearby Chattanooga to both large department stores to find the best piece. In the children's section in Loveman's, she found a splendid white silk gown with collar brocade and an embroidered cross at the front neckline. She announced to Granny that they had found it! It was said that Mom's excitement over this Wesleyan find was somewhat tempered at each step along the way toward purchase by Granny's downcast expression, deeply projected sighs, and martyred agreement with "I reckon that'll do" as Mom strode toward the clerk's counter.

Family speculation was that Granny had always viewed *me* as the reincarnation of W. T. Millwood. This transcendental outlook on Granny's part would explain her obsessive love for me, her efforts to place a grandmotherly protective shield around my every move, her almost angry reaction to my dad's and uncles' rounding me up for trips to see the Chattanooga Lookouts minor league baseball team play, her spending as much time with me as she possibly could, and her constant worrying that I would get hurt or worse, even when I simply left the house in the morning for the safe walk to school. Now that I think about it, her hovering over me would explain the mysterious disappearances of my Daisy BB gun, a treasured pocket knife, and my new boxing gloves. These items were instruments of the devil, of course.

Obviously, Granny had wanted me to wear W. T.'s christening gown, had her heart set on it, in fact. But Mom could see no way that W. T.'s gown could be reconditioned by the christening date. One early spring day three weeks before the big event, Mom came home from work and with unusual determination ushered Granny into the living room. Mom sat on one end of the couch; Granny settled into the nearest chair. "Mama, we've got to agree on this thing," my mom began. "I know how much you loved little W. T. I wish I had known my brother. But he's been gone a long time, and his christening gown hasn't aged all that well. You know it. You don't want Mike to go through that ceremony wearing a gown that'll look dirty and wrinkled no matter how much we work on it. Why, Annie Corley'll whisper all over Post Oak that we didn't do right by this sacrament. Aunt Lattie'll fume and spew and cuss and criticize us for years after this. And what'll we say to Aunt Clarice and Uncle Jasper when they come down from Chattanooga in their big ol' Lincoln expecting to see everything perfect and we give'em a dirty lookin' christening gown? Now we both know that this christening isn't about appearances—it's about Mike's commitment to the Lord—no, don't interrupt me, please—but we ought to dress him up as nice as we can in front of all the church and our family. Don't you see, Mama? Let's make it as special as we can. OK?"

Granny had been avoiding Mom's direct gaze by eyeing the large pastoral painting behind the couch for most of the time Mom was talking. When Mom finished, almost worn out from her speech and tiptoeing on eggshells in her effort not to hurt her mother's feelings, Granny said, "You know, Francine, that ol' picture behind you's kinda yellowish and hangin' crooked. I need to clean it and straighten it." She noticed Mom's raised eyebrows and angry disbelief in this change of subject, so she quickly continued, "Yes, honey, I reckon we should use the gown you bought. Yes, I reckon we should. Bless your heart. You always know the right thing to do." But Granny wasn't convinced.

For some time following Mom's earnest plea to Granny, things went too well, a sure-fire warning in my family that all hell was on the verge of breaking loose. It did.

All of us arose from bed at 6:00 a.m. on the sacred christening day. Then it all moved apace: from the quickly prepared breakfast of pancakes and bacon and coffee to the laborious process of dressing for church and especially of dressing me in the fancy new gown to the impatient dealing with three lengthy, reverse-charge, long distance phone calls from two great aunts and a cousin. One of the main events I wish I had seen involved Granny's effort to stay warm. It was a sunny but quite cool day in northwest Georgia, and my grandmother needed to be warm in between the different phases of her donning of the underthings and dress and hat—and her hard decision about a purse. She dominated our one small bathroom for a long, long time that morning, finally emerging only after the wonderful thing happened that was chronicled for years at family gatherings.

It seems that Granny instituted her habit of backing up against any source of warmth—a steam radiator, a coal oil furnace, a fireplace—so that she could receive the effects of the soothing heat slowly covering her body. Her butt was required to be the absorption point for most of this heat. In this case, she backed up to the small electric wall heater in the bathroom in her usual back-stepping, shuffling manner. Two items are worth note: this little heater could really generate the hot stuff and Granny had just a moment before pulled on and fastened her girdle. The girdle and bra were phase one of the dressing process, and, to this point, nothing else had been put on. But she needed to warm up. Not long after Granny had assumed the rump-extended-to-the-rear position and begun to feel the welcomed warmth, she started to smell something that reeked of burning rubber. Outside in the hall, Mom smelled it, too, and called, "Mama, what's that smell? Are you all right? Did you get a plastic hair roller caught on the heater grate again?"

My grandmother didn't need Mom's update. Granny realized she was way too close to the heater. She knew also that the interesting smell came from the girdle's rubber lining and elastic edging literally melting away. "Whooo-eee! Ouch! Ouch! Ouch!" yelled Granny as she jumped from the heater's grid, leaving most of the girdle stuck to the heater and the imprint of the grid on her now pink and naked buttocks. At this point Mom rushed in, moved her mother further aside, turned off the heater, and waited for the girdle remnants to burn off or to pretty much become as one with the heater's steel cover.

"Are you hurt, Mama? Do we need to call Dr. Cookman?" Mom was stressed now as the time approached for the family's short walk to the church, but she was more concerned about her mother.

"I don't need a thing, thank you. And I ain't hurt? Red's got to fix that damned heater. The coils get too hot, can't you see? It wasn't my fault." Indignant and embarrassed, Granny covered herself with a towel, grabbed up some toiletry items, and stalked to her bedroom. Dad watched her out of the corner of his eye, but he knew better than to laugh.

This became one of those family legacies that gets funnier and funnier in the re-telling over the years. One version even had Granny stuck to the heater, mercifully no longer blazing heat, until my mom and Mrs. Corley could un-stick her by rolling washcloth-covered ice cubes over and over the melted mess. It took a good while. Annie Corley laughed while Granny cussed. Another version related by Uncle Herman, though he wasn't an eyewitness, reported that the Post Oak Volunteer Fire Department was called to put out the "famous girdle fire of 1948" after Granny extricated herself and ran out of the house holding fast the bath towel representing the only covering she could find. Of course my grandmother denied all of this.

You'd think we'd had enough excitement this day. Not so. Granny was to provide still more.

Following the great girdle burn and the remainder of the family's dressing for church, we fortunately still had almost thirty minutes before the two-block procession downtown should begin. Time for a last cup of coffee. Granny, having ushered into service a second-string girdle, had somehow managed to recover some—but not all—of her dignity in preparation for the occasion and had walked over to my crib to peer down at my blessed little self. I was half asleep—but fully bathed and dressed in the striking new christening gown from Loveman's. She began her usual silly baby talk with all of the attendant phrases: "Look at this sweet thing! Ain't he just the prettiest thing you've ever seen? He's my precious little angel. Yes, he sure is." Then she would make this clucking sound while she stroked my head and patted my fat little legs. And all of this would've been OK except for one issue.

You see, Franny Millwood, my stellar and always proper grandmother, was given to an infrequent pinch of snuff tucked discretely, usually, just under her lower lip. On this morning following the girdle incident, she had deemed it necessary to use the snuff to steady her nerves before church. In most cases, she could talk with the snuff in place without anyone noticing. But the clucking sound of endearment changed the rules a bit. With the second wave of clucking, a slight dribble of brownish liquid oozed from her lower lip and dripped three or four times onto the neck area and front brocade of my gown. Granny moved back out of snuff range when she realized what she'd done (Until her dying day, she proclaimed the snuff dribble was totally accidental.) and turned to yell at Mom. "Francine, I've done made a mess here. Come help me. I didn't mean to do it! We can take care of it, I think."

Mom took four or five steps over, immediately saw the gown's changed ambiance, and proceeded to move into conniption mode. In the South we know about conniptions and tantrums and hissy fits—as opposed to behavior related to one's being merely pissed off. One typically loses her/his dignity and sense of conscience during a conniption. One screams and stomps. One's face contorts. One might generate spittle. It just happens. Mom lost her composure and scolded Granny without remorse. "Mama, how could you do that? You use that damned dirty ol' snuff and make messes with it. But how could you get close to Mike with that stuff on this morning of *all* mornings? Now you've ruined everything! What are we a-gonna to do now? Just tell me that! Whatever are we a-gonna do?" She ran off to her bedroom and slammed the door. Dad comforted me because the disturbance had called up my oft-used sequential litany of timed screams: "Wah . . . wah . . . wah . . . !" My contributions added a nice audio touch to the family preparation.

Granny disappeared for a couple of minutes into her room and came out holding another gown. Of course it was W. T.'s. But this one was not wrinkled or damaged or stained at all. It wasn't pristine, but it was beautiful in its own right and demonstrated an early 20th century seamstress's care and precision and best work with cloth and needle. Holding the carefully ironed piece next to her chest, she walked to the closed door of Mom's room and softly said, "Francine, come out and see this. I think W. T.'s gown'll work all right. I worked on it a lot over the last few weeks, just so's I'd remember. I think it'll work. It ain't as pretty as the Loveman's gown, but it'll work."

Mom slowly opened the door and stood in front of Granny. My mother was quick to temper sometimes, but she always regretted it when she'd lashed out at one of her family, especially her mother. And at this point, with time running out, she was desperate. "Let me see it," she said, holding back tears. Mom turned it over a couple of times, felt the all-too-familiar fabric, and held it out in the light for a better view. "Mama, how in the world have you managed to clean this gown up to look so nice? It used to be a disaster. I think it *will* work. Thank God!" The two of them hugged briefly. Somehow, on that sacred Sunday, forgiveness did abound, and the gown substitution was not mentioned again that day.

The christening ceremony itself went well, for the most part. I didn't particularly like it when Reverend Morris took me from Dad at the altar, dipped his right hand into the baptismal font, and gently sprinkled the water over my head. I think I raised hell a bit, too, when the preacher, holding me in front with both hands, stepped forward to present me to the congregation, but I was generally forgiven for knocking off Reverend Morris's glasses and for trying to bite his hand. I can only hope that the Lord was willing to overlook these little expressions of anger on His day of receiving honor and another member of the flock. I'll find out, I suppose, when St. Pete opens the ledger on me.

Both gowns now reside in an old antique trunk in our guest bedroom. The Loveman's piece was never cleaned or used again. The snuff stain is still there on the front, a tribute to a strong-willed and loving woman whose family and church meant the world to her. And whether the snuff dribble was accidental or intentional, Granny remained blameless as the christening gown story was re-told over the decades. With grandmothers, that's how it should be, I reckon.

Dad and the Cattle Car

The Christmas when I was five was my all-time favorite Christmas. Santa brought me that year an .027 gauge Lionel electric train with Erie twin diesel engines, a Sunoco petroleum tanker, a coal hopper, a yellow cattle car with operating doors (my absolute neatest car), a log carrier, and a deep red, lighted caboose. Enough three-rail track was included for me to have a looped figure eight layout, two or three billboard and track warning accessories, and a solid piece of plywood for a platform that enabled all of this to be mounted and stabilized. I also received a Roy Rogers cowboy outfit dangling with fringe, a double six-gun holster, a coonskin hat (Davy Crockett was big that year, but the linkage with my 1940s Roy Rogers outfit was historically questionable.), two or three toy trucks, a football, and a small blackboard with chalk. And this was just the basic Santa stuff. Other family members loaded me up with books, plastic army soldiers, a silver tin B-17 that made a loud whirring noise and spun its propellers when you pushed it along your make-believe runway, new shirts and jeans, a 1/25th scale Corvette sports car (The real thing had made its debut that year.), and a few still shiny silver dollars from my wealthy great aunts from Chattanooga. What a haul!

Before you get the wrong idea, we were certainly not the richest folks in Post Oak, Georgia, in 1953. Far from it. My good gifting fortune at Christmas—and at birthdays, at Easter, even occasionally on just regular weekends—was based on my status as the first kid to come along in my family in a long, long time. The result was my becoming spoiled—but I never took anything for granted and never let them know I was spoiled. Spoiling has to do with expectations, and I always camouflaged my expectations.

My mom's family was the group I remembered most vividly during my childhood. My maternal grandmother lived with us until her death when I was ten. She was probably the chief spoiler. Mom had two older sisters, both of whom were married but without children at the time. These aunts and uncles seemed to enjoy taking me on trips and loading me up with all kinds of toys and sports items and were always important people in my young life. This was good.

On the other hand, my parents were not very well off and struggled to make a go of it. They both worked outside the home, a circumstance you didn't usually see in the homes of my buddies in Post Oak. While not living the *Leave It to Beaver* semi-affluency with a daily bejeweled June Cleaver as a parent, my friends had mothers who were almost all stay-at-home moms. My situation was not the same. At different times, Mom was a data processor, an assistant in the county tax assessor's office, and a hospital insurance clerk. Dad was a small- town grocer when small towns had such things as small-town grocery stores and, later, a supermarket meat cutter. And all would have gone well except for my dad's ongoing and sometimes serious problem with the bottle.

Keeping a steady job became a real challenge for my dad much of the time. We lived in rental houses and moved a lot, something I didn't really understand until I was in junior high school. At the time, I didn't even grasp enough to be embarrassed by our situation, but I now realize that paying the rent and other bills on credit—and getting behind on payments—resulted in Mom's constant effort to put people off, not answer the phone occasionally, and play the stressful game of "robbing Peter to pay Paul." But I reckon all of the family shielded me from these more difficult issues, so I just continued merrily along with my primary and selfish concern of begging enough money to buy baseball cards and model World War II planes. Maybe it was better to be oblivious to this living-on-the-edge lifestyle anyway.

This incident is about Dad more than anything else. While he spent many years drinking up paychecks, losing jobs, and driving Mom to distraction with his errant ways, he was still a decent, good humored, intelligent, kind hearted fellow. He loved me and was, in his own way, proud of me although he never could quite find the words to tell me. It was easy for all of us to love Red Lockhart and to become extremely put out with him at the same time.

I can't recall right at the moment whether Tom Brokaw discussed examples like my dad in *The Greatest Generation*. Probably there were many. Growing up in the Depression and surviving World War II in Company B of the 794th MP Battalion in Italy with Mark Clark's Fifth Army no doubt influenced my dad in ways he didn't choose to talk about. From a number of family stories, I learned that my dad developed the habit of drink in his twenties when he lived with his oldest brother's young family in Chattanooga, the large city 18 miles to the north of Post Oak. And he took that habit with him when he enlisted in the Army in mid-1942 following his becoming aware of his 1-A draft classification. He went on to complete basic training at Camp Pendleton, California, and a short while afterwards went overseas with a Tennessee National Guard unit.

Dad's troop ship's first port was Casablanca followed quickly by travel to a place in the south of Italy in the Tyrrhenian Sea. While anchored in a small harbor awaiting debarkation, Dad's ship was torpedoed by a Nazi, or perhaps

Italian, U-boat that had managed to slip under the submarine nets. When the torpedo hit, my dad was topside for a cigarette, having just climbed up from the hold and away from a torrid poker game. The troop ship was breaking in half. Dad and some other guys ran to the splitting section and looked down through a crunched and crumbling mass of steel that had previously served as a gangway. Water was rushing in and over the guys in the hold. Some had already drowned and were floating with macabre expressions of terror with eyes and mouths open. Others coughed and spluttered and flailed their arms as they tried to forestall the horror of drowning. Some had been brutally struck by pieces of shrapnel from the exploded torpedo and were scared and bleeding and screaming, delirious with pain. According to Dad, all of this happened so fast that nothing much could be done to save the soldiers in the hold. Their part of the ship sank quickly; the part my dad was on stayed afloat long enough for about two-thirds of the guys to be rescued. Until the day he died, Dad had nightmares about those drowning young men, a few he had known back in Chattanooga and most of whom had been Dad's basic training buddies in California.

All in all, Red Lockhart was a study in contrast. He was one of the hardest working men I've ever seen, yet he would not go to work sometimes or arrive late because his hangover was too painful. Then he would be reprimanded by his boss, followed in due course by the habitual increasing rage. The result, as he was wont to say, was his usual refrain as he explained his recent unemployment to Mom: "Dammit! He can't talk to me that way! I took off my apron, threw it down, and walked out." This frequent show of pride was something we could ill afford. He could be a committed, loving husband and father, yet he would often find a local bar after work on his weekly payday and cause a major dent in the rent and car payment. He would devoutly promise Mom that he would curtail the hard stuff and, indeed, stay off the bottle for weeks, yet I would sometimes find her sitting on the edge of their bed in tears, holding an almost consumed half-pint of Old Crow whiskey that had been hidden under his laundered shirts in the chest of drawers.

He often counseled me on a man's obligation to be fair, to do the right thing, to honor his word, to show courtesy, to act in an ethical manner. Heck, he was the one who taught me to move to the outside, near the traffic, when I walked down the sidewalk with a lady. Yet I learned through one of my aunts that Dad had won Mom's hand in marriage by violating an agreement not long after most of our Georgia and Tennessee guys had returned from the war. It seems that Dad, who ended his military career a private first class, and Martin Munroe, a Post Oak native and serious-minded infantry captain, had both courted my mother before the war in person and during the war by correspondence. Martin had gone through school with Mom in Post Oak; my dad had met her in a bar one pre-war Saturday night in Chattanooga. Oh, my!

After the war, this interesting triangle heated up. Dad and Martin agreed at one point that they would both stay away from Mom for one entire month to allow her to think carefully about what she wanted to do. The Captain of Infantry, a man of true integrity, kept his word. My dad waited for two days into the agreement period, called Mom, and went to her house with an engagement ring. I think the date had been set before Martin Munroe learned of his loss. I suppose all is fair in love, war, and post-war courtship agreements.

Dad would complain occasionally about a couple of younger guys he worked with because of their slack work ethic, unreliability, and mean treatment of their families, even chewing these fellows out as their supervisor after he had once been promoted to manager of a supermarket meat department. Then, one day when I arrived at the store to pick him up (The three of us juggled our work schedules around one car, and I was often the designated taxi service.), I found him under a jacked-up car in the back parking lot. He was installing brake shoes on the piece-of-crap car belonging to one of the slackers. Mom later learned that he had also paid for the brake shoes. It's not surprising that he regularly completed tax returns for both of these guys because they were unable to read well enough to follow the IRS instructions.

Once for Christmas he presented Mom with a beautiful and somewhat expensive necklace from a fancy jewelry store in Chattanooga. She was stunned and cried in joy for days. A year or so later he was required to hock the necklace because we were way behind in our bills. And the beat went on.

The episode with the cattle car falls under this listing of contrasts, I think, and is a fitting tribute to the core Red Lockhart. It's important to know how very much I loved and appreciated my Lionel train on that age-five Christmas—and afterwards. I played with it for hours on end. You see, in addition to my simply loving the train because it was so neat, that train gave me standing among my group of Post Oak buddies. They all wanted to be around it and work the transformer and see the accessories operate. The log loader and dispatch station were especially popular. Only one other guy we knew was lucky enough to have a Lionel layout, and he was a lot older than we were and wanted little to do with us.

I think my parents also embraced the train gift because, once the train had become an important Christmas tradition, the train set could be added on to with fascinating accessories each time Santa visited. This situation cut down on the adult creativity—and probably expense—associated with Santa's yearly visits. Now I was not always able to have the train assembled and play-worthy given our tendency to move from place to place and occupy houses of limited square footage. But usually Dad would help me find a place, set up the plywood platform, take the diesels and cars out of their boxes, assemble the track and connectors, and ensure that everything worked OK.

Some family events in the South are forever etched in memory and talked about around the Thanksgiving table and front porch ice cream churnings in the summer. You know how it is. Such was this event the Christmas two years after Santa initially brought the train. We lived in an old, spacious house then, and I was allocated plenty of room for my train layout. If my memory serves correctly, this episode took place on Christmas night of the Santa visit which brought me two side-rail switchers and a flagman's house. Lionel provided such wonderful accessories then.

My layout was in complete working order. And at night I enjoyed turning out most of the lights in the train room, turning on the transformer, and lying down on the floor near the tracks to watch the Erie diesels come around a curve with headlights fully on and the click-clack of the wheels announcing yet another approach. Occasional sparks would jump out when the diesel locomotive crossed a slightly loose track joint. My prone position gave me an eye-level, head-on view of the train, and when it neared, I could reach back to the transformer's red lever with my left hand to sound the horn. From time to time, I would trade out or remove certain cars because I had grown my freight train's size to the point where my use of all of my cars strained the motorized diesel's power. On this night I had taken off my splendid yellow cattle car and my coal hopper complete with a load of tiny Lionel-manufactured coal. By this time, my cattle car even held five in-scale cows that could barely be seen through the car's realistically constructed, open spaced side planks. But I knew they were there, by golly. Both of these cars were now off the train platform and on the floor about six feet away from my skinny, stretched out little body. On this night the offloading procedure for these cars created the venue for this etched-in family experience.

It didn't take Dad long to get tight once he'd begun to drink. While he consumed the Old Crow in private, he had no reservations about bringing in a couple of six-packs of Sterling Beer in front of his family. He would open each can with our old "church key" can opener, appear to relish the fizz, and toss back the beer. After the third one or so, depending on how much supper he'd had, he'd be slurring a little and talking ever more loudly. After the first six-pack was history, he'd stagger when he walked to the bathroom, a trip made often. When he'd moved well into the second six-pack, he was looped enough to have his coughing spasms and walk in a decidedly irregular, uncertain pattern from room to room. He appeared always, for some reason, to be listing to port as he staggered along.

Thankfully, he usually spent most of his drinking time at the kitchen table across from Mom, who dutifully sat with him for hours on end, worrying about the effects of his beer on his chain smoking habit and his tendency to light up in bed, despite all of her fussing. But Mom wasn't at the table on this particular post-Santa night. A few other family members were in the house, though, including one of Dad's older brothers, Fred, from over toward Macon. Fred could hold his own with Dad where drinking was concerned, and he and Dad were both at the kitchen table enjoying a bit of post-Christmas cheer well beyond the ideal stop time for any holiday happy hour. The last strains of Bing Crosby singing *O Little Town of Bethlehem* wafted through the house and somehow didn't fit with the shared drinking, coughing, and occasional belching at the kitchen table.

I didn't really care much what was going on in the kitchen or the *Christmas with Bing* album because I had discovered a better way to stop my log loader car beside the log loader accessory, unload the logs to the bottom of the conveyer belt, move the car up to the load point, and watch the logs move upward, pause for an instant, then individually roll down and into the waiting loader car. I guess it never occurred to me that this exercise in unloading the logs and re-loading the same logs into the same car at its slightly more forward location was a rather pointless task. You have to wonder whether the Lionel folks consulted government officials in my adopted state of South Carolina to come up with the concept for this accessory. But, nah . . . you don't worry about this kind of thing when you're six or seven.

I left the log loader and had already moved on to the idea of placing my flagman's house over closer to the loader so it'd look as if the flagman were there to slow the train down and prepare for the log loading work. By the way, some of you Lionel enthusiasts will remember that this flagman accessory was a little house designed to be located near your track. As was the case with most Lionel accessories, a clip connector drew power from the rails and operated this lighted small structure. When the train approached, a special piece of track would engage the flagman accessory. The door to the house would open, the flagman would come out on a sort of camouflaged track in the house's base, he would swing his red-tinted lantern, and then he would disappear back into the house. I never tired of watching this part of my railroad world. When you're seven years old, your personal universe is a grand thing, free of substantial responsibility and decision-making and requiring so little for entertainment.

I must've been still engrossed in all things railroad when Dad entered the room that night. His sluggish, listing stagger was not at all quiet, but the constant click-clack of the speeding train coupled with Bing's cheery baritone voice masked his entry. He had moved fairly close to me when he began, "Hey, ol' Buddy Boy (His nickname for me was Buddy.), whatcha doin'? " Startled, I sort of jumped and turned to see him. As he greeted me, he slightly lost his balance and raised one foot up and down to the side to stabilize himself. This deft maneuver might have worked without casualty, but the balancing foot in question unfortunately landed smack dab in the top center of my yellow cattle car.

During my childhood, Lionel trains were always quality pieces of American manufacture, and they survived much rough play imposed by thousands of little junior buttholes like me. But the weight of a grown adult male finding exactly the "sweet spot" of the top of an .027 gauge cattle car was too much even for this durable accessory. You could hear the crunching sound as the little train car resisted but then gave in to the heavy footfall. Dad had also knocked over the coal hopper and scattered the miniature pieces of coal everywhere, but no collateral damage was done to this car. I jumped to my feet and gazed with horror as Dad stumbled away from the scene of the devastation and awkwardly grabbed at a wall. I slowly took the two steps required to reach the now smashed car. Then, with hopeful denial, I groped for the overhead light switch.

Full illumination revealed the worst. The solid, thick plastic sides had splintered into many, many yellow pieces, some lying around the platform and a few others bent to the side of the floor of the car. Three of the cows had survived. Two others had lost heads and legs in the accident, body parts that were strewn throughout the wreckage.

"Oh, no," said my dad. "I'm so sorry, Buddy. . . you know I didn't mean to . . . hic . . . didn't see the car here in the dark . . . hic . . . wouldn't have done this for anything in the world." He actually seemed to sober up a little as he looked around, not knowing really what to say or do.

"It's OK, Dad. It's an accident. You couldn't see it. It's all right." As I think back over this incident, now over sixty years in the past, I'm glad I managed not to cry, and I'm glad I didn't lash out in anger. I moved back to the transformer and turned everything off. "I'll get to this stuff tomorrow," I remember saying. "I think I'll go to bed now." I sadly looked up at Dad, and, as he surveyed the room before him and turned back to me, I saw an expression I'd never seen before. I said nothing else. One last time I looked back at the yellowish pieces and parts and made my way down the hall to my bedroom.

The next morning I slept in. School wasn't set to start back for another eight days or so, and I wasn't much in the mood to meet the day with the expected glee over the recent Christmas bounty. When I did return to my train room, I was surprised to notice that everything was put back in order. The coal hopper was righted with all the coal back in. The cattle car mess had been cleaned up with no hint that anything bad had even happened. And that was the kicker, I recall thinking. Nothing of the cattle car remained next to the platform: no splinters, no cow parts, not even the pretty much undamaged chassis and road wheels. It was all gone. I supposed that Mom had come in, swept up, and thrown away the debris. Oh, well. Maybe I can get a cattle car replacement next Christmas, I thought. And Santa surely won't let the replacement count against my normal Yuletide stash.

Time's a funny thing when you're a kid. Sometimes it drags on and on, like when it's 2:15 in the afternoon at a small town grammar school and you're waiting for the 2:45 bell to ring signaling the mass exodus to the parked busses and to the walking line-ups for the town kids. It didn't help a bit that a large wall clock resided above the green, cursive letter, instructional placards over the blackboard. The minute hand wouldn't move at all if you watched it. And if you tried to pass the last thirty minutes by re-reading your most recent *Weekly Reader*, you couldn't possibly regenerate interest in the silly raccoon cartoon or the article about an archeology expedition to Mongolia. On the other hand, if you'd gotten involved in a good after-school, pick-up baseball game over at the American Legion field and a bunch of the older boys were playing, too, it seemed like only fifteen minutes had gone by before it started to get dark. Damn! Time was never a kid's friend when the kid was six or seven years old.

As I waited out the Christmas holidays during that winter of 1955, I couldn't seem to find fun in anything. My new bicycle was OK and fantastic to ride, and the Ft. Apache cavalry set was great to set up in the living room. I could even combine the cavalrymen and Indians with a couple of cabins from my Lincoln Logs set to create an intriguing Western combat experience. And I appreciated my plastic British Spitfire model plane, but I assembled it quickly, played with it indifferently for a little while, and put it back on the dresser in my room. For some reason, I couldn't get back to my first love: the train platform and the excitement of my rumbling diesels and freight cars and flagman and track switchers.

I went into the train room only twice over the next eight days, neither time assuming my squatty position near the transformer, ready at a moment's notice to lie flat in the dark to watch the train rumble toward me. Now that I think about it, Mom and Dad didn't ask me why I wasn't playing with my train. They didn't say much to me at all. I reckon it's a totally different dynamic when either the Mom or the Dad somehow screws up instead of the kid. You know, when this kind of thing happens, it's incumbent upon the kid to get the most out of it. If you handle it right, you might get an increase in allowance or a trip to Lake Winnepesaukah or even two more model planes. The secret, though, is not to make them feel too guilty. Down that road lies a full rejection of things you might need because they get really upset and embarrassed and avoid you. Better to strike the balance between reasonable imposed guilt and the acknowledgement that you're a decent enough kid to let them off the hook—at some appropriate point. I don't want you to get the wrong impression about me, but I'd pretty much mastered the parental guilt trip business by the time I was seven.

Somehow, though, I didn't work it on my dad during the two weeks following the smashed cattle car episode. I just couldn't. He looked downcast enough when he was around me and didn't talk to me much at all. Then one day, after I had been back in school for a week or so following the holidays, Dad was waiting for me when I walked into the house. He was sitting in the living room with a cup of coffee (Coffee was a constant staple in my house then with its pleasing Maxwell House aroma and homey sound of china clinking when it was poured.), and he got up to come over to me. I had just put my small book satchel and ball glove down on a chair when I noticed him. Dad began, "Buddy, let's go into the train room for a minute. OK? I wanna show you somethin'. I can't make up for breakin' your train car, but I really wanna try."

They had already raised my allowance to seventy-five cents weekly from its previous largess of fifty cents, and they had thrown in a fancy new metal basket to fit on the handlebars of my bicycle. I didn't need to press it. "OK, sure," I replied. I had no idea what was in store, but from Dad's expression and from the fact that he was home early from work and from his sobriety, I figured it might be good.

It was dark enough in the train room for Dad to switch on the overhead light. The platform, train, and accessories emerged slowly from the light and looked almost new to me again. Dad looked down at the platform, his eyes directed toward the fully connected freight train now back on the tracks from my previous soft rebellion of placing all the cars off to the side, like I didn't care anymore. It was meant to tell them that I was still grieving for my cattle car. It's the subtle things like this that really get to them.

I quickly took stock until I saw the new yellow cattle car positioned as the last car before the caboose. "Man!" I almost yelled. "It's a new cattle car. Thanks, Dad! I can't wait to get this thing runnin'!" This new car, in fact, held four plastic cows and two pigs this time, none of which were quite in scale, but that didn't matter at all. Dad had remembered this detail. Most kids would probably have hugged their dads right at this point, but we didn't have that kind of relationship. Instead, I looked up at him, kind of nodded, grinned, and jumped into my full-play, squatty position next to the transformer.

Almost as an afterthought, Dad reached behind one of the legs of the platform to bring out another car. I paused a moment from my headlong drive to engage the train to see what he was handing me. He stammered, "I . . . uh . . . uh . . . figured the base, wheels, and couplers of the old cattle car were still good, so I've . . . I've tried to use them to make you another car. You don't have to couple it to the rest of your train . . . it might be too tacky . . . but anyway . . . here it is."

I hurriedly got up, took this extra car from him, and looked it over. I realized that Dad had cut a piece of what looked like balsa wood to fit exactly onto the top of the old car's chassis. This new base was painted brown, as were what I then saw were wooden stakes rising from the sides of the car, six of them in all. They nestled precisely into equidistant notches cut into the wooden floor. Maybe the neatest things of all were the six "logs" being carried by this special log carrier. I knew—because I had seen Mom remove them prior to putting on a roast for Sunday dinner—that small wooden dowels were sometimes inserted into certain cuts of meat, especially roasts from the Red Food Store, to support these special cuts, I supposed. They were tied together at times with butcher's twine. Dad had commissioned six of these dowels into service as logs, and, to be truthful, these dowels were only slightly larger than the Lionel logs that came with my log loader accessory. They would probably even fit on the conveyor belt of my log loader. My new logs were stacked in a 3-2-1 arrangement starting from the base, and they looked so realistic.

I was too eager to affix this car to my waiting train to consider the creative thinking and time my dad had invested in this project. As I recall, I reassumed the squatty position holding my new log carrier, disconnected the Lionel log car and coal hopper, coupled Dad's car between them, and turned on the transformer. The Erie diesels began their work of pulling my newly augmented freight cars. The homemade log carrier was indeed different from the other factory-produced, shinier-than-thou Lionel freight cars, but I didn't care. This log carrier possessed qualities no other of my cars would ever possess: the love for me and of atonement. As the old Miller Lite commercial used to proclaim, "Hit don't git no better'n this!" I noticed Dad again only as he stepped toward the door to leave me at play, and my notice was quick. I looked at him and smiled; he smiled back and slowly nodded his head once. Then he left the room.

My dad died of lung cancer on Christmas Eve in 1972. Mom succumbed to the same disease on New Year's Eve in 1988. They were both taken by the "disease *du jour*" of their time brought on by addictive smoking. My old Lionel train has survived many moves, both during our lean times when I was a kid and during my working career on active duty in the Army and as a college faculty member and administrator. My train now resides on top of an old English glass-front cabinet in our home office, a cabinet containing numerous memory pieces from my wife's family and mine. The train doesn't run now although I threaten around Christmas time each year to take it to our local train hobbyist shop to have it reconditioned.

A horn is broken off my front diesel, the paint from several cars has chipped in numerous places, and ladders have fallen off my tanker car and my coal hopper. The transformer and what's left of my power connectors don't work. Most of the metal stakes have long since disappeared from my original Lionel log carrier. But, you know, those six wooden stakes Dad installed on my makeshift log car still wait proudly to hold those dowel logs, dowels sadly long ago misplaced or thrown away. The emptiness detracts little from this car. And this homemade log carrier now sits on two pieces of rusty track immediately behind my diesels on the old cabinet, ready, it seems, to join my freight rig should I set up my reconditioned outfit around a future Christmas tree.

Ah, well . . . maybe next Christmas . . .

Loaded Up at the Load-em Up

"Y ou white trash heathens have gone and done it this time! You've took my precious angel to that horrible cesspool of sin like I warned you never to do! Now you've done it! You're all goin' straight to hell!" Granny was over the top.

It didn't happen often, but sometimes, as a kid, I came face-to-face with the potential for sin and corruption. I never completely succumbed—I don't think—because I had too many—far too many—saintly grandmothers, aunts, great aunts, female cousins, Methodist circle members, and my mother watching over me. But I needed at least the possibility of corruption. Heck! Life's no fun without it. One of my favorite memories speaks to my crouching at the precipice of what Granny feared was my full-fledged tumble into the downward abyss of Dante's hell.

My grandmother's diatribe was aimed at my dad and two uncles on Mom's side. Her harsh words followed our late-night arrival at home from a minor league baseball game and a wonderful experience at a honky-tonk near Chattanooga, Tennessee. It seemed to me and my unfledged Methodist education that the consignment to hell was small consequence.

The Load-em Up Tavern was located just over the Georgia-Tennessee line into the Volunteer State only about five miles south of the Chattanooga city limits. The tavern was actually in Westview, Tennessee, even in the 1950s a beginning-to-thrive suburb of its much larger metropolitan neighbor to the north. This place was a touch above seedy and not a dangerous dive for guys in my home of Post Oak, Georgia, who sought to escape the perils and misfortune of living in a dry county.

It helps to know that the Load-em Up had been built in 1950 on the site of an old, raucous, 1920s roadside tavern. Today, interestingly enough, you can still see its footprint if you drive past on Highway 41. On this same spot, a stately, nicely steepled Assembly of God church now greets those who speed by on their way through Westview to Chattanooga. As late as 1992 and to acknowledge—and perhaps to lay to rest—the site's previous not-so-pristine reputation, the church leaders posted on their marquee this sign with almost an Old Testament flavor: "Where sin did once abound, now faith doth here abide." Clever, huh? This kind of church marquee poetry is still big in northwest Georgia and southeast Tennessee.

My dad and both of my close-in uncles frequented the Load-em Up on occasion but not so often as to qualify for any volume discounts. The distaff side of Mom's immediate family—to wit, her two sisters, Aunt Lucinda and Aunt Rebecca—had married two fellows who had worked in the same large engineering company in Chattanooga after the war. Coincidentally, Uncle Tom and Uncle Herman set their sights on Mom's sisters at almost the same time and pursued their goals almost simultaneously. This was probably a convenient arrangement: think of the savings realized by car pooling on dates, for one thing. In the process, they got to know my dad, also a veteran and who had, two years earlier in 1946, married Mom. My parents' union of hearts followed Dad's underhanded victory over a local World War II infantry captain who had also sought Mom's hand in marriage.

My dad and two uncles got along well, enjoyed weekend time together, and especially relished holiday occasions when our family could celebrate the season and delight in my grandmother's cooking. For some inexplicable reason, they all three enjoyed my company. Well, Dad sort of had to—he was obligated. But Uncle Tom and Uncle Herman weren't quite as obligated, and they still seemed to like me. I reckon, since neither of my uncles had children at the time, they saw me as a surrogate kid not always underfoot who dearly loved becoming the subject of attention of these sports-minded, toy and baseball card buying, joke telling, roughhousing, and sometimes rough talking guys. Life sometimes doles out these lucky circumstances, you know.

One Saturday afternoon in mid-July, Uncle Tom and Aunt Rebecca came over to the house for a visit and, if things worked out, some home churned ice cream. Dad was on his way home from work, and Uncle Herman was tuning up his lawn mower at his house, as I understand it. Aunt Lucinda, Mom, and Granny were already established at the kitchen table and were on their second cups of coffee. Upon walking quickly through the front door (Doors weren't ever locked then, and no one bothered to call before coming over.) and taking in the full situation, Aunt Rebecca almost tripped over Amos the cat in her rush to the coffee pot. And I was over at Will Weaver's place trading ball cards and shooting BBs at Coke bottles set up on an old wash tub. The result of all of this was that no males were at our house when Uncle Tom showed up with Aunt Rebecca, and the prospect of a lengthy gossip session with all of these Millwood women was not appealing to my uncle. It's the chance you take when you don't recon the sector before driving over. TV wasn't an option, either, because Uncle Tom's choices included reruns of *December Bride*, a flower arranging program from Nashville, or a documentary about the dying gasps of Joseph McCarthy's anti-communism witch hunts. The baseball game-of-the-week had been rained out, and, in 1956 in our television viewing area, the game options and any game backups due to rain were non-existent since ESPN and its derivatives were decades in the future.

Always a man of quick wit and keen reason, Uncle Tom decided hastily that the women weren't about to conclude their discussion any time soon, especially since word was out that a state legislator from Marietta had run off with Commissioner Quinn's wife. This sort of thing needs comprehensive scrutiny and careful speculation about outcomes. It might even require occasional telephone updates from Mrs. Sweeney, the weekend phone operator, who waited with bated breath for an inquiry from someone on one of her party lines. This party line system was more effective and more personal than our current social media venues, I'm convinced. But Tom Massengill intended to have no part of this intense "current events in Post Oak" discussion. Instead, he figured, Red, Herman, and I will take Mike to see the Lookouts play! And we can stop back by the Load-em Up for a cold one on the way home. This'll work well, he thought.

Uncle Tom's plan was too special to me to go unexplained. You see, the Lookouts were the Chattanooga Lookouts, for years a double A minor league affiliate of the Washington Senators and residing in the old Southern Association. For those who care, other Southern Association teams in the 1950's included the Atlanta Crackers, the Birmingham Barons, the Memphis Chicks, the Mobile Bears, the Nashville Vols, the New Orleans Pelicans, and the Arkansas Travelers. I was lucky enough to be taken to see the Lookouts play several times a season, usually by one of my uncles. Never do I recall a time when all three of my main adult males joined forces to take me to a game. This was great!

As is often the case, when something promises to be too good to be true, the promise almost never works out for everyone involved. Now Uncle Tom's plan worked out fine for me. But I'm uncertain that it worked out so well for my dad and uncles. Most assuredly, what these gentlemen wanted to avoid at all cost was a confrontation with my grandmother. Down deep, I think, she loved all three of her sons-in-law. I think. But she pretty much ruled the roost in our family. Sadly widowed in the mid-1930's, she lived with us and took care of me after school because both of my parents worked. She controlled the extended family's social calendar, if such were said to exist. She was the front person for any juicy Post Oak gossip and shared it freely with her daughters and Methodist circle friends. She was the primary meal preparer on all holidays. She stood smack dab in the way of most extracurricular celebratory goals—involving alcohol—concocted by Dad, Uncle Tom, and Uncle Herman. She still attended local meetings of the Woman's Christian Temperance Union (WCTU) at our church and took pride in her staunch invectives against the terrors of demon rum. She always maintained an overriding suspicion regarding any special trips I might be invited to take with my dad and uncles. She didn't trust those guys with me at all. But there's more to it than lack of trust, I reckon. I've decided through the years that Granny obsessed over me so much because, in some way or other, I had taken the place of her first child and only son, W. T. Little W. T. had died at age five in 1918, a victim of the horrible influenza epidemic that ravaged the world. Many in the family used to say that Franny Millwood never got over W. T.'s death, and, indeed, she was apparently comforting him with her last words on June 18, 1958, the day she died.

When Uncle Tom announced his intention to round up his brothers-in-law and me to take this fun-filled drive to Engel Stadium in Chattanooga to watch the Lookouts, Granny was adamant: "I know what's a-gonna happen. Y'all will get in the car and go to town and see that game. You'll leave and come back through Westview and stop at that sin-infested place, that Load You Up, or whatever it's called. And y'all will probably get drunk. And my precious angel will be there to see all that! No, I ain't a-gonna stand for it. No, sir, ain't nobody gonna take little Michael to any place where they drink beer and play cards and talk dirty and roll dice and shoot pool and play that awful pinball machine and commune with floozy women. You heathens know better'n that. It ain't a-gonna happen, I tell you!"

Uncle Tom rose from the couch and placed his right arm gently around Granny's shoulders. "Franny, you know we ain't a-gonna subject this little feller to any kind of co-ruption. Why, Red wouldn't stand for it, first of all. He plumb wouldn't stand for any kind of bad stuff happenin' to his only son. We just wanna see the game and give Mike the chance to go, too. You know how he loves the Lookouts. Come on, now. Don't you worry 'bout us. Everthin's gonna be all right. I gar-an-tee it. We'll be back early. We won't go near the Load'em Up. OK?"

"Damn it to hell!" Granny interjected, using one of the three obscene expressions she even knew. "Tom Massengill," Granny emphasized as she pulled away from my uncle's loving hug, "I swear I'll beat you till the cows come home if you let Mike be a part of any of those bad ol' things you boys do. You know I mean it." She finished this admonition with her right index finger wagging in a sword-like position about two inches from Uncle Tom's nose.

Uncle Tom was a big man, probably six one and around 215 pounds. He had played on a good high school football team in the mid-thirties, had attended Georgia Tech for two years before the war, and had been part of an aeronautical and ordnance team that worked to refine the successful, for its time, Norden bomb sight used on most of our heavy and medium bombers over Germany and Japan. But he was no match for Granny—nor did he wish to be. "Now, Franny," he started, "don't you worry . . ."

"Don't you 'now Franny' me, you trashy thing. I know what'll happen. And I don't like it one bit. Rebecca, Francine, ain't y'all a-gonna do anything 'bout this?" Her voice rising to peak shrillness, Granny was on the verge of one of her classic hissy fits.

When neither Mom nor Aunt Rebecca stepped forward to intervene, Granny issued a loud "harrumph" and stomped loudly back toward her bedroom. You could hear "Those worthless hooligans, those trashy tramps, those heathens" as she made her way down the hall. I knew Uncle Tom had won the skirmish, but the full-scale battle was far from over. Then her door slammed, and the drive to Engel Stadium finally loomed large.

The four of us enjoyed our time that evening. The game was OK, but the Lookouts lost to Birmingham 8-3. During the time our team was affiliated with Washington, the Senators regularly fielded the worst team in the American League. When the major league team's season had gone fully to pot—usually by the end of June—the Washington general manager started calling up good players from the minors. Over time, as I recall, the Lookouts lost the likes of Jim Lemon, Harmon Killebrew, Jim Kaat, and, a bit later, Ferguson Jenkins through these mid-season call-ups. Even if the Lookouts were competitive, we all knew it was just a matter of time before our two or three best players would leave, we'd receive replacements from some Class B club in Toad Suck, Arkansas, or some such hotbed of baseball talent, and we'd see the Lookouts rapidly descend to the second tier of the Southern Association. Crap! But there was more to my evening with my adult male role models than just the score of the game.

Uncle Tom drove that evening. He always seemed to have a new Pontiac, and I looked forward to my opportunities to ride with him in this nice car with the Indian head hood ornament. And there's something special, you know, about that exciting new car smell, even in 1956. I was usually allowed to ride in the front seat between my uncle and Aunt Rebecca; this time I was up front between Uncle Tom and my dad. "I think Minnick'll start tonight," said Uncle Herman from the back seat. "He's good when his curve's a-workin', but he's lost three in a row since the series with Mobile last month."

Rhetorical grunts of agreement came from Dad and Uncle Tom. Then, to change things up a bit and test my ongoing memorization of major league statistics, Uncle Herman asked, "Mike, what's Ted Williams hittin' now, and how many homers does ol' Duke Snider have?"

I answered both questions correctly with something like, "Williams is at .328, and Snider hit his 22nd homer yestiddy 'gainst the Cubs." This isn't to brag, but I read the sports pages religiously back then, moving first to the box scores and on quickly to the league leaders in all hitting and pitching categories. I could memorize all the statistics with little trouble. But there were only 16 teams then in all of major league baseball.

This statistical saturation needs elaboration. One of our worthless Clark cousins, Andrew Ray, the one who went AWOL after only a few days of basic training at Ft. Benning and hid from the MPs under our kitchen table, used to escort me to the barber shop at haircut time. Granny at first appreciated Andrew Ray's care and concern, but then she discovered the truth. Her nephew would make book in the barber shop on my current knowledge of baseball stats, knowing that I had read the sports pages in the morning *Chattanooga Times* in advance of the sports scan by any of the riffraff in the shop. I almost always won these baseball stats contests, and Andrew Ray knew how to turn my knowledge into *his* gain. One Thursday he won $18.50 from the assemblage, including the barbers. For my trouble, Andrew Ray gave me enough money to buy six packs of baseball cards and a chocolate milkshake from Dr. McEachern's Drug Store. It seemed like a good deal at the time. Andrew Ray told me never to tell Granny about "the little game" we played with the guys in the barber shop.

But the day after my cousin's $18.50 take, I let it slip that I had finally gotten Willie Mays in a new pack of cards and that Will Weaver would really be jealous. Astute at keeping up with all the sordid details of my life, Granny realized that I had already spent my allowance that week and she hadn't provided any extra money to support my baseball card habit. Upon thorough interrogation, I came clean about Andrew Ray's giving me the money following the little game in the barber shop. When I said that the game started when Andrew Ray took money from the shop customers and wrote down some amounts in his small notebook, Granny's face turned red, and she seemed to know about the game and how it was played. The next time he showed up at our house, Granny ran him off the porch with her broom brandished above her head as if it were a medieval broad axe. Andrew Ray didn't come around for a long time.

But my experience going to the Lookouts game is more important than this other stuff. Each one of us got a program, and Uncle Herman taught me how to track the game on pages that looked sort of like box scores. That was fun! I remember enjoying a lot of popcorn, a hot dog, two candy bars, and a Coke during the game. On the way out, Dad bought me one of those miniature Louisville Slugger bats that baseball franchises sold in their souvenir shops. Now, you can see that I had already done well, but I had no way of knowing what else was in store for me that night!

Uncle Tom had lied to Granny. We *did* stop at the Load'em Up—and stayed there until almost midnight. When we were first getting out of the car, Uncle Tom gave me a dollar and told me to go next door to Fallow's Rexall Drug Store and buy some ball cards and candy. I did and came back quickly. Dad and my uncles were sitting on some stools at a counter right underneath a fancy glass case which displayed an old red wagon pulled by six large, light brown horses. A neon sign under the case blinked out this slogan: "Budweiser—the King of Beers." I really liked that wagon and horses and said so to the guy behind the counter. He smiled, sort of, promptly ignored me, and slid a tray with several foam-heavy beers on it down the counter to a woman wearing a skimpy short skirt and a pretty doggone tight blouse. Uncle Herman then saw to my need for the evening meal. While Dad and my uncles talked with some of their buddies, like Frank Saverance and Tater Patterson and Cotton McAllister, I ate a wonderful fried chicken basket and slurped down two bottle Cokes.

When I'd finished off the last drumstick, I was taken by Uncle Herman over to this long, slanted table that sported all of these blinking lights and bells and ping noises and color pictures of these girls with mermaid tails and very little to hide their top parts. They were nestled into a tall, grassy area surrounded by sand and palm trees. Sailors in white uniforms watched these gals with supreme interest. The slanted part ended at a seventy degree turn where another part of this machine formed a back wall with even more color illustrations. All of this was under thick glass. I remember it pretty clearly. God knows, I would have a lot to tell Will Weaver the next day.

Then I watched a guy put some money into the side of this contraption, wait until a stack of silver balls rolled down close to where he was standing, and pull back on a lever that had a spring action to it. When he turned loose, the other side of the lever hit one of those balls, and this ball went blasting up a kind of ramp and out toward the top of this machine. The guy became really excited then. He jumped up and pulled and released some other side levers so that he could control the ball's movements from side to side and up and down. His best efforts would engage these flapper devices toward the table's bottom which would send the ball back where it came from, striking the pegs and increasing the point count. I realized that each time the ball hit a certain peg or chrome cup, the bells would ring again and an increasing total points read-out would glow. Obviously, the object was to keep each ball in play for as long as you could. Eventually, though, the guy would miss, and the ball would roll down to the bottom near the player and into another hole, not to be seen again during the game at hand. Then another ball would position itself in front of the power lever, the player would pull back and release the lever, and the next ball's journey would begin.

When all the balls had moved through their back and forth trips down the table and finally into the exit hole, the player gave out with a frustrated "Damn!" and turned to the beer pourer at the counter. "Hey, Drummond," he said. "Did I win over ol' Tater over there? I think I'm top dog right now."

"You're over 150 points short, Max," the bar tender replied. "You'ins can see the top score over to the right of your score. See? Don't gimme no crap 'bout winnin' when you can see your score on the machine. You'ins want another beer?"

"Hell, no," was the rejoinder. "I'm gettin' outta this cheatin' place. I think you've rigged this damn machine to keep the scores low. I'm a-gonna talk with the Westview police tomorrow, and they'll make you 'splain how you can fix the scorin' and why the house ain't never lost."

When this pissed-off guy left, Uncle Herman told me it was my turn. He found a small stool, positioned it under the front of that marvelous machine, picked me up, and balanced me toward the front of this strange slanted table. He reached into his pocket and pulled out a good bit of change. "OK, Mike. See where I'm puttin' the dime? You do this then pull back on this here lever right here. This'll make the balls come down, and you can play. Got it?" Uncle Herman was setting me up for a long play at the machine, maybe enough time to see him and Dad and Uncle Tom through two more cold ones apiece.

Well, I'll tell you, I had some fun that night! Maybe my lack of arm strength caused my initial thrust of the ball to leave the ramp with added control or maybe the high point pegs were among the first the ball would hit if not madly speeding out of the blocks or maybe it was just blind luck. Heck, I don't know. But I do know that I would keep each ball in play for a long time, that the mermaid tails seemed to wiggle each time I maneuvered a ball into a tight channel, that the pings and bells and lights became addictive (if such could happen with a little eight-year-old junior munchkin), and that my point totals vastly exceeded Tater's and the pissed-off guy's who played before me. Between dimes, I could see Drummond talking with Uncle Herman and quietly passing my uncle a wad of money. Uncle Herman would take the cash, smile and nod approvingly toward me, wave his arms to encourage me to keep on playing, and order another Budweiser. I noticed a little later that several customers were watching me, grinning, and, once or twice, even applauding. If cousin Andrew Ray had been around, he'd probably have moved out around the tables, taken out his notebook, winked at the drinkers, taken some money, and started writing down some stuff. Then I might have ended up with a huge stash of ball cards. But one shouldn't be greedy, I reckon.

We left for Post Oak after I'd played for about an hour. It was a quarter of twelve. Dad and my uncles were all a little tight, but Uncle Tom was driving slowly enough to be safe and not to attract any attention from the county's finest. I was sleepy and moved over to put my head against Dad's shoulder. He patted me, moved my legs up onto the seat, turned me a bit, and brought my head down into his lap so that I could stretch out on the front seat. This was special because Dad wasn't given to this kind of closeness. The three of them were talking pretty excitedly about the evening and especially about my skill at what they were calling a "pinball machine." Uncle Herman said something about my dad putting some money into my savings account at the Bank of Post Oak. I didn't understand, but it sounded OK. As we passed by the Post Oak city limits sign on the north end of town, Uncle Tom suddenly put on his blinker and pulled erratically into the Barbeque Shack parking lot. "Whatcha doin' this for, Tom?" Uncle Herman asked.

Uncle Tom was really upset. "Guys, we're a-gonna catch hell in roughly ten minutes. Ain't nobody gonna be asleep in that house, bet on it. Franny'll be a-waitin' at the front door. God a-mighty! She's a-gonna have a 'Come to Jesus' session with all of us and then with each one of us individually. What're we a-gonna do?"

"Take our punishment, I guess," said Dad. He was slurring his words a bit but was still able to be clear about the situation. "Y'all have wives to pick up, I've got to open the store in the mornin', Mike needs to get to bed, and Franny just might be so glad we're safe that "you Godless heathens" might be the worst we'll get. Let's just go on home."

We did. And it would have played out pretty much the way Dad had predicted. But my excitement got in the way, sort of like it did with cousin Andrew Ray and the bookmaking on baseball statistics in the barbershop. Uncle Tom counseled me as we drove into the driveway *not* to say anything at all about the pinball machine: nothing about my standing on the stool to reach the controls, nothing about the mermaids and sailors, nothing about the bells and pings and lights and points, nothing at all. I certainly had the best of intentions. Even at age eight, I had enough sense not to want to mess up a good thing like going to see the Lookouts and visiting the Load-em Up afterwards. And, Lord knows, I had already been the subject of several of Granny's hissy fits during my young life and didn't enjoy seeing those things—even if they were aimed elsewhere.

Granny regaled her sons-in-law royally as we four entered the house. "Heathen" and "white trash" were at the top of her list of preferred titles as she went into the faces of all three of my male role models. She even removed her small wad of

Bruton snuff from inside her lower lip, so this was obviously a serious matter. Dad quickly excused himself to go to the bathroom, a sanctuary from which he would not have wished to emerge. It occurred to me that maybe I could distract Granny and give Uncle Tom and Uncle Herman a chance to escape with their wives—and lives. I picked up my sack of baseball cards, candy, the score books, and the souvenir bat from Engel Stadium and rushed over to show these treasures to my grandmother. Unfortunately, I hadn't noticed that ol' Drummond—good ol' Drummond, the tavern owner and bar tender—had dropped in several trade cards with beer advertising clearly visible and, perish forbid, a note he'd written to me on a piece of a Load-em Up notepad. Granny saw the beer ads first, threw them to the floor, commandeered the note, and read out loud—slowly—to everyone there gathered: "To my youngest and best pinball wizard, Mike Lockhart. Come back any time, little guy. The stool will always be ready for you, and all of my mermaids will be wiggling their tails in your honor." At this point, Granny gasped and clutched at her heart. She continued to read, "In a few years, I want the chance to buy you your first Pabst Blue Ribbon. Best regards, your friend, Drummond. P.S. Tell your Granny I said 'hi.'" This P.S. was the kicker, I think. Fifteen years earlier, Drummond's phone calls to try to get my widowed grandmother to spend some social time with him went unheeded and, in fact, were rebuffed with strong words. She had no use for the owner of a honky-tonk in Westview, Tennessee. In her view, I'm sure, any time she might have spent with Drummond would have revoked her WCTU membership. Perish forbid! She looked up from the note, her eyes narrowed, and she clenched her teeth, an act made more convenient without the presence of snuff.

While finishing the note, she had begun to multi-task. She had been reading to us and backing toward the front door at the same time, deftly blocking any exit route my uncles might have sought. Stopping, she called loudly, "Red, you come outta the bathroom right now. You've had time to pee six times. Get out here!" Dad sheepishly opened the bathroom door and joined Uncle Tom and Uncle Herman in the living room. Probably able to be given a "pass" from what was about to happen, even so, I stepped over to these three men and prepared to take the punishment, too. I felt really grown up, having spent several hours at the ol' Load-em Up. Granny looked at me and said, "Mike, you go on to bed. I'm a-gonna say some things to your father and uncles, and you don't need to hear me. Go on, now."

"No'm," I answered in a shaky voice, barely believing what was coming out of my mouth. "I've been bad, too, and you need to cuss me along with them. No one made me play the pinball machine, not Uncle Herman and not Mr. Drummond. I played it, and I really enjoyed it. And I guess that means I really enjoy sin, if that's what you think it is. But if it was sin, it really was fun!"

Somehow, without understanding it, I had presented this good Methodist woman with a significant theological dilemma. She could rationalize that, if I had been practically kidnapped by these three hooligans to go to Chattanooga and to the Load-em Up, I wasn't at fault. Her "precious angel" was blameless, without blemish, without sin. Just like little W. T. But if the angel admitted his guilt, his sin, even becoming proud of it and reveling in it, then there was a contradiction, a theodicy, of sorts. These two things can't exist together: Mike is without sin, but Mike has just admitted to sin and seems to like it. All of Granny's scripture readings and all of the Post Oak Methodist Church and its sermons and Sunday School classes had failed. Granny, for one of the few times in her life, was stumped. After a moment or two of reflection with her head down and still holding Drummond's note, she looked up at the four of us. "Y'all get away from me right now," she said.

"I ain't a-gonna continue this conversation with Mike feelin' the way he does 'bout what y'all done to him. We'll talk about this tomorrow. Mike, I'm disappointed in you. I got to think."

I didn't want Granny to be disappointed in me, but I didn't want to be one of the targets of a hissy fit either. I'd seen those. I went on to bed.

Three or four days later, I asked Dad whether Granny had crawled him about our trip to Chattanooga. "Naw, buddy," he said, "she hasn't. I know she hasn't forgotten about it. I guess she's got a lot of other stuff on her mind right now." We all had begun to notice a few odd quirks in Granny's behavior that would eventually lead to her confrontation with dementia. Dad spoke kindly: "I want you to be especially nice to her for a while. OK?"

"Yeah," I agreed. And, you know, I think I *was* pretty good for a long time. Why, I didn't even take advantage of my usual method of getting extra money from her for ball cards. Sometimes she'd lose her glasses and ask me to help her find them. I'd normally agree to help, ask her for the routine twenty-five cents for five packs of cards, and then tell her with a snicker that her glasses were pushed back on top of her head. But following the Load-em Up episode, I made it a practice to just point to her forehead, smile, and go on out to play without holding out my dirty hand for the quarter. It was kind of my gesture of love and penance. The first time I declined the previously extorted money, I remember walking down the front steps, stopping, and quickly turning back toward the house. Granny was watching me, smiling. I smiled back. The making of family peace is a good thing.

I wonder what Uncle W. T. used to do for spending money.

The Parakeet and the Preacher

I n my house, we all owned our own Bibles: my grandmother, my mom, me, and probably even my dad (although he never admitted to it and I saw him thumbing through what looked like a Bible only once to check a crossword puzzle clue). All of us stored important keepsakes in our Bibles, stuff like gems of printed life wisdom cut from the "Focus on Religion" weekend section of the *Chattanooga Times*, pressed four-leaf clovers, pages from *The Upper Room*, book markers for the 23rd Psalm and John 3:16, and, as it happens, dropped feathers from any one of a number of family pet parakeets. These little birds were popular during my childhood.

On one particular day I wished to re-read the Parable of the Prodigal Son to ensure the rightness of what our Sunday School teacher had just said. The father's joyful celebration of the return of the boy who had left home and wasted his inheritance didn't make sense to my fourth grade grasp of things. I also found myself aligning with the older son who had stayed to work the farm while the prodigal ran wild in Vegas. I just didn't get this lesson about forgiveness, I reckon. So as I carefully opened my personal King James Bible to Luke 15 and turned one page, a green and yellowish parakeet feather floated softly into my lap. The feather had belonged to Aunt Rebecca and Uncle Tom's parakeet, Bobby, and was gifted to me by Aunt Rebecca probably at around the same time I received my Bible from Mom during the summer of 1956. I held the feather gently, recalling my times with this intelligent, mischievous little fellow and the fun we had. Don't be snide. One found one's entertainment wherever one could find it in mid-1950s North Georgia.

Several things in my kid memory bank that I consider special include my baseball cards; my plastic model World War II planes; Little League baseball; our Friday night shopping trips to Chattanooga complete with a restaurant meal of tasty fried trout; MYF sessions on Sunday nights; my parents' canasta games at our kitchen table with their good friends; frugal vacations to Panama City, Florida, called at one time the "Redneck Riviera"; cutthroat family Scrabble games at Aunt Rebecca and Uncle Tom Massengill's house; paint-by-number sets; the baseball *Game of the Week* with Dizzy Dean and Pee Wee Reese on TV; and my extended family's collection of fascinating pets. One of the grandest of these pets was the heretofore mentioned Bobby, a phenomenal parakeet whose verbal skills outpaced those of a number of my fourth grade buddies. I'm not proud to say this; it's just the way things were back then.

After all this time and following my visits to many, many pet shops where large bird cages held colorful parakeets, canaries, a few cockatoos, and an occasional parrot, I'm certain that Bobby was, by far, the smartest bird in a large tri-state area. I was allowed to let him out of his cage when I visited my aunt and uncle, and he was accustomed to me and my small right index finger when it served as his perch. In fact, when any familiar human came to his cage, he would run up and down his perch and engage in a frenetic bird dance of bobbing and shaking his head sometimes accompanied by whistling and loud chirping. And this show of excitement would often forecast an outburst of clear parakeet conversation.

He never flew away from me during our times together. When I affectionately offered my fingers, ears, lips, and nose, Bobby would lightly nip the offending body part with his beak kept partly blunted by means of the cuttlebone attached to a couple of inside bars of his cage. He never drew blood.

He would stand on the edge of my plate when I consumed one of Aunt Rebecca's ham sandwiches. He watched patiently from my shoulder as I assembled a plastic model plane or tank on the large desk in the guest bedroom/office. As soon as enough of the model would be finished to provide a different perch, he excitedly sensed the opportunity. He would hop to the desk's surface, waddle over to the fuselage or tank hull, then awkwardly climb to a place on the model where he, even with his diminutive stature, would most assuredly be in the way of my assembly. He had planned this, I'm convinced. I would halt the process, realizing that any aggressive and unattended squeezing of glue could result in a tiny bird foot becoming as one with the tank turret or number two engine on the B-17 bomber. When he was certain that I had caved to his work stoppage tactic, he would hop into the box of plastic parts, decal sheet, tiny paint brushes, and bottles of paint and begin to pick up and throw out of the box any loose items he could manage to lift, stuff like landing struts, turret hatches, extra track sections, even, one time, a vertical B-17 tail section (quite large for a bird similar in scale size to the Geico lizard). This was all OK. It was fun to watch. I could always finish my model later after Bobby had been returned to his cage and a bath towel gently spread over his home to enable the little guy to enjoy a peaceful night's sleep. But, you know, this little feathered gremlin wasn't always asleep underneath the comforting towel. No, sir, not by a long shot. He was still plotting.

The success of this ornithological remembrance relies on an important feature of Bobby's precocious personality and smartness. Many parakeets can mimic human voices, I'm told, but few could do so with Bobby's aplomb, volume, articulation, and clarity. Bobby didn't squawk out his words scratchily and parrot-like—he didn't have to. He could be well understood through background noise across the room, and sometimes he could lift his message from one room to another.

By the third year of his adoption by Aunt Rebecca and Uncle Tom, Bobby had acquired a vocabulary of over thirty words along with a number of phrases—even complete sentences—he could use at will. His favorites included "Bobby's a pretty bird!" "I want a beer!" "Piece of toast!" "Put me down!" "I thought I saw a puddy cat!" (Uncle Tom worked a long time to perfect this one.) "I'm Bobby; who are you?" and "Candy, candy!" Bobby's loquacious talents cropped up unpredictably and not always in context. And his substantial lexicon didn't stop here. Some of the other words and phrases were taught to the bird by Uncle Tom and a few of his buddies during Friday night poker games at Tom's house. We'll come back to this later.

Bobby always attracted admiring glances and compliments from anyone visiting in the Massengill home. He relished this praise, moving across his perch closer to the admirer and rubbing his head on the bars closest to his new friend. Bobby was not at all shy. Indeed, he was very much enjoying the attention on the day the Susanna Wesley Circle of the Post Oak Methodist Church met at Aunt Rebecca's house for refreshments, a devotional, a business meeting, and conversation with the newly assigned minister, Reverend Barton Copeland.

This circle meeting drew interesting attendees. First, Reverend Copeland was a serious, pious, caring young man of thirty-five or so, married with an attractive wife and two-year-old daughter. He carried much memorized scripture on the tip of his tongue and wasn't reluctant to recite these holy words. As the circle's special guest, he was seated with his back toward Aunt Rebecca's living room picture window and only three paces or so away from Bobby's cage and cage stand. Aunt Rebecca sat to the preacher's right and a bit closer to Bobby's cage. This turned out to be a good placement, I reckon.

Ten other stalwarts of our town's Methodist Church completed the circular seating arrangement with, of course, everyone's line of vision directed toward Reverend Copeland.

To the preacher's immediate left was Ruby Trendle, a slightly overweight and neatly adorned and graying lady in her late fifties who basked in her role as Susanna Wesley Circle President. Basking was a strong feature in Ruby's life. She basked also in her solo soprano position in the sanctuary choir, as well as in other church committee slots, and no conversation with Ruby was undertaken without two or three reminders from her that it would be difficult to open the doors of the Post Oak Methodist Church without her. You know the type.

Marlena Danforth, a small and sadly meek lady, sat next to Ruby. She would hang on Ruby's every word and incline her head toward her friend even at the mere hint that Ruby was about to speak. Marlena was infatuated with anyone, such as Ruby, who was educated and in a position of authority, so the circle's having Ruby in charge with Reverend Copeland in their midst was almost more than Marlena could bear.

A sofa end table came between Marlena and the next attendee, Miss Fancy Emmons, one of the longest-tenured circle members. She was the most senior English teacher at Post Oak High School. Miss Emmons, as she insisted to be called, was formal at all times, officious in her manner of talk, and judgmental to a fault. Anything that departed from her strict view of propriety or from *Robert's Rules of Order* during any kind of meeting would be met with her harsh rebuke. The last time she laughed, it was said, occurred many years before around the turn of the century when her sister fell from a seesaw and broke her wrist during recess at the Post Oak Grammar School.

Six other Susanna Wesley Circle members sat around in the loosely assembled collection of dining table and living room chairs in this proper Methodist gathering. My grandmother attended, too, but the only other member in need of specific mention was Patsy Jaytree, the wife of the owner of one of Post Oak's small grocery stores. She was a bit younger than the other circle goers and new to the church social and administrative culture. She wanted so much to please and to say and do the right thing, but this effort at correctness usually escaped her. When it did, she often reacted with an embarrassed, spontaneous laugh that was too loud and raspy and punctuated with what sounded like interrupted belching.

The on-stage setting for this circle drama has now been established. What needs more elaboration is the off-stage piece that made this Susanna Wesley Circle session the talk of Post Oak for over a year following its playing out. And you'd never guess that Uncle Tom's innocuous poker games established this off-stage part of the drama.

On at least two Fridays a month, a few of the stellar citizens of Post Oak would gather at the Massengill house for late-night poker. The "usual suspects" included Uncle Tom, of course, along with Sheriff Samuels; Curley Raeford, who owned the Gulf Station south of town; Jimmy Allen Walker, the main proprietor of Walker Brothers Furniture Store; and Shorty Macintosh, who had recently bought the Western Auto franchise on Cleburne Street. These fellows arrived near seven thirty and planned to stay around until well after midnight. The large, bright yellow, Formica kitchen table became the site for these torrid contests of will and risk. Aunt Rebecca wasn't overly fond of these high-toned civic sessions in her home, but she tolerated the tradition and even provided a round or two of small sandwiches and chips and her famous brownies. An expected treat occurred also as each player took his seat. By this time, Uncle Tom and Jimmy Allen had opened a large cooler full of iced-down Budweisers. Jimmy Allen, in fact, frequently employed his rusting church key to open the first cans of Buds and pass the beverages around.

But the particulars of the poker games matter less than the contribution the town's finest made to the previously described Susanna Wesley Circle meeting. You see, following the first hand of the evening and each participant's throwing back of a couple of cold ones each, Uncle Tom would take Bobby out of his living room cage and bring him in to join the card game. Aunt Rebecca watched over her little pet closely, but, by and large, she trusted the guys to enjoy the parakeet and ensure that he didn't get hurt. Truth be known, Bobby would get excited to see these familiar fellows come together in the Massengill house. He would chirp loudly and run up and down his perch, occasionally sharply pecking his mirror and bell for more sound effect and attention. Then he often enunciated rapidly, "I want a beer! I want a beer!" probably wishing, no doubt, to be considered just one of the guys.

He jumped to Uncle Tom's index finger when the cage door opened. His first treat was to slurp his own beer from a small porcelain dish Uncle Tom kept for just this occasion. The citizens all liked this feature of the evening, believing firmly that no other poker group in Landsford County could boast of a feathered mascot with a taste for suds. Later, after Bobby had consumed enough of his own bird beer to become a bit tipsy and quite gutsy, he would waddle to each player, yank a card or two from each hand, and display the cards, always face up, on the table. This habit signaled the near end of Bobby's appearance at table, but he wasn't returned to his cage until the language lessons had taken place.

Uncle Tom led this procedure, with Sheriff Samuels and Shorty Macintosh closely involved. In brief, Uncle Tom would encourage Bobby onto an index finger perch, move the bird close to one of the language instructors, and begin the session.

A LIZARD, A PARAKEET, AND A METHODIST GRANDMOTHER

Bobby was a quick study, in need of little drill and practice. When he'd picked up a word or phrase in his bird pea-brain, the recent learning was there, by golly! Shorty was deemed responsible for the "I want a beer!" admonition, while the town's high sheriff was blamed for Bobby's "What a party! What a party!" and the "You're a juicy gal! Juicy . . . Juicy!" demonstrations. Even so, no one owned up to the clearly pronounced term that rankled the Susanna Wesley Circle and closed down the poker games for a long time. With due apology, this term, repeated with gusto by the feisty parakeet, went this way: "Shit, Bobby . . . S *** . . . s *** . . . s ***." The repetition provided an especially nice effect to the bird's vocabulary achievement. Somehow, this part of Bobby's lexicon was kept from Aunt Rebecca, but not for long.

It's no mystery how the circle meeting, the introduction of the new preacher, and the parakeet's newest vocabulary acquisition played out. On this delightful day, Aunt Rebecca first directed her friends to the refreshments, managed to get everyone properly seated, and asked the chatty circle members for attention: "Ladies, before we eat and begin our meeting, I'd like to introduce our special guest, Reverend Barton Copeland. He and his family moved into the parsonage only three weeks ago, and he graciously consented to come to this circle meeting as he gets to know his flock. Reverend Copeland, we're thankful for your presence with us."

The slightly nervous young minister rose to acknowledge Aunt Rebecca's kindness and emphasized his appreciation for the invitation and for his opportunity to meet these good Post Oak Methodists. He even smiled and nodded back toward Bobby. "I'm honored, also, to have in our midst one of God's special little creations. We recall, don't we, the meaningful words from the hymn, the reminder that God gifts us with 'all creatures, great and small.'" This good young man was to rue his reflection dearly.

54

Aunt Rebecca took the opportunity to use Reverend Copeland's status among the group to ask him to return thanks. He said, "Of course I will. First let me add my deepest appreciation to you, Mrs. Massengill, for your willingness to receive us into your beautiful home. Now, if you will bow with me."

No one had noticed that Bobby was beginning to express substantial interest in the goings on in his typically calm and unoccupied living room in the middle of the day. He had moved to the end of his wooden perch and as close as he could get to the gathering with the tall man now standing and speaking softly next to Aunt Rebecca. No one—and not even Aunt Rebecca—had noticed Bobby's interest and the initial twitching of his little bird dance.

Following a brief pause for spiritual effect, Reverend Copeland began, "Gracious God, we truly do treasure this time together. The ministry represented by these dedicated circle groups of women, long a Methodist tradition, is indeed a strength of our faith and enables the commitment of one to be multiplied by the commitment of many." He paused again, longer this time to fold in the pious agreement of these adoring women. No one indeed—and not even Aunt Rebecca—had noticed this time that Bobby's little body was leaning left then right in a sort of bouncing, rapid bird strut and that his head was bobbing up and down. He was getting really wound up. So far, no sound had come out.

The preacher continued, wanting his prayer to extol the benefits of the circle system before he provided the obligatory blessing of the food. He prayed a bit louder, "So how can we praise Your work and Your purpose through these good people, O God? What should we say?"

Bobby answered the somewhat rhetorical question, with clear enunciation and appropriate volume: "Shit, Bobby. S *** . . . s *** . . . s ***!" How the little guy was able to match his phrasing to the exact context of the moment was never understood. But he did.

This one demonstration of Bobby's extensive language skill was later attributed to Uncle Tom and Shorty Macintosh, but they both pleaded the fifth. Whatever the origin, Bobby got off two more iterations of his message before Aunt Rebecca, stumbling in her desperate lunge to the standing cage, could grab the towel, cover the cage, remove the cage from the stand's hanger, and shuffle quickly back to her bedroom. Aunt Rebecca later told Mom that she considered opening one of the bedroom windows, climbing out to her car, and driving away, not stopping until she had reached Birmingham or maybe Mobile or even Dallas. She would call a lawyer later to deal with Uncle Tom. But to her credit, she shook her head, wiped her brow with one of Uncle Tom's handkerchiefs, and returned to the living room in time to hear Reverend Copeland's "And we ask these things in the spirit of the Christ, Amen." The only addition to the closing "Amen" was Patsy's unfortunate and inappropriate belch-laugh, but no one seemed to notice.

In the best display of Methodist loyalty, empathy, and love for the remainder of that Susanna Wesley Circle meeting, no one referred to Bobby's augmentation of Reverend Copeland's blessing. Ruby Trendle assumed her role as circle president and presided through the meeting's agenda. The circle's business went quickly, for once. The attendees were anxious to finish their business and depart Aunt Rebecca's house, with as little repartee as absolutely necessary. The anxiety over Bobby's exclamations remained icy and palpable in the living room. These folks wanted out. Everyone even seemed to forget the need for a benediction.

Following adjournment, Marlena Danforth and Patsy Jaytree offered, almost insisted, that they help with the post-meeting clean up and dish washing, but Aunt Rebecca politely yet firmly declined. One of her intensive migraines was rapidly approaching, and she needed total quiet and isolation. As the last two ladies were leaving with Reverend Copeland in tow, Aunt Rebecca smiled and thanked them for coming. She assured the new preacher that she and Uncle Tom would see him on Sunday. This was a lie, of course, because, as she stood at the door, Aunt Rebecca was already deciding on the slowest and most painful way she could kill her husband, how far away from Post Oak she could get before the body was discovered, and whether she could count on Mom's legal support, her mother's, and my Aunt Lucinda and Uncle Herman's.

Not to worry. There was no dreadful murder in my family that day following Uncle Tom's normal return from his engineering job in Chattanooga. But there was a lengthy, specific counseling session waiting for Uncle Tom along with Aunt Rebecca's conducting an in-depth post mortem leading to conclusion of the Friday night poker games. According to Uncle Tom, her uninterrupted diatribe was punctuated with terms that put Bobby's colorful addition to the preacher's prayer to shame. This was not something a fine Southern lady should be proud of, but, well, one must do what one must do.

When the rest of the family learned of the circle fiasco, the first reactions came in the spirit of sympathy and understanding. Granny, who was a witness to the event, had lingered following the circle's break-up and consoled her eldest daughter as best she could. According to the debriefings from the event, Granny's worst condemnation of Tom Massengill was, "That trashy ol' thing shouldn't have them no-good men over for those sinful poker games. He'll owe you a lot for a long time, honey. Don't let him off the hook! Bless your little heart."

After Aunt Lucinda had told Uncle Herman about Bobby's intervention in the circle meeting and after Herman had stopped laughing, she scolded him harshly and reminded him not to bring up the matter at the next family Sunday dinner. Uncle Herman and my dad were true to their pledges to be mindful of Aunt Rebecca's embarrassment, but Tom Massengill wasn't as thoughtful. He'd always relished opportunities to tease Aunt Rebecca and to chuckle heartily at his wife's expense. But these jabs were good-natured and loving.

Finally, that Sunday after dinner when everyone had adjourned to the Massengill living room, the site of the recent bird vespers, Aunt Rebecca broke down and laughed with the rest of the family as she provided more details about the aftermath of Bobby's completion of Reverend Copeland's blessing. She was very effective at emulating Miss Fancy Emmons, who left the circle meeting with her cold, judgmental comment of pious closure: "Rebecca Massengill, you've always been a Christian martyr to put up with that nasty husband of yours and those heathens who gamble at your house. Maybe now you'll force Tom to schedule an appointment with Reverend Copeland and begin—begin, mind you—a return to the Lord." She had left in righteous indignation.

"This return will take a long, long time, you know," added Dad, "and Bobby's language won't get any cleaner in the process."

Everyone laughed.

Uncle Herman leaned over and gave his sister-in-law a hug. "Rebecca, I'm glad you're now seeing the humor in this here thing. Why, I ain't had this much fun since the hogs ate my sister." At this, Aunt Lucinda pinched Herman hard on the leg. He yelled in pain. All of us laughed at his reaction and in mock agreement with his assessment.

Then we heard from the parakeet cage in the corner, "I want a beer! I want a beer!" Granny shook her head and waved a menacing finger toward Tom.

Aunt Rebecca leveled her threatening stare at her husband then resignedly brought out the small porcelain dish, poured a tiny quantity of a previously opened Budweiser into it, and carefully placed it on the floor of Bobby's cage. The slurping seemed louder and happier than usual.

Somehow, Bobby was never blamed for his outburst. The messenger isn't always killed, I guess. As for Reverend Copeland, he never broached the subject of the circle meeting with Aunt Rebecca. Her atonement of agreeing to play the piano for hymns at the Sunday night services was sufficient penance.

AWOL in Post Oak

Every Southern family has one. Our cousin, Andrew Ray Clark, was ours. I'm referring to that composite of a true eccentric, a self-absorbed butthole, and a black sheep.

Andrew Ray was the youngest son of Aunt Lattie and Uncle Sim Clark. He was considered from high school to be a strange and unlikable kind of boy, always cutting up, blowing off school work, playing jokes on his older brothers and classmates, disrespecting and smart talking almost all elders, showing a penchant for remarkable laziness, stealing money from his own mother on occasion, and constantly buttering up his aunt Franny—my grandmother—to have her cover for him so that he could get by with stuff at his own home or around Post Oak.

He was always looking for an angle. A few times, when I was eight or so, he took me to get a haircut. He really wasn't being helpful to my family. He knew I loved baseball and, on a daily basis in the summer, had memorized all the statistics for the batting and pitching leaders in both leagues. Andrew Ray would challenge the guys in Markson's Barber Shop to try to outwit me in my statistical knowledge. He would embarrass the barber shop patrons with condescending challenges: "Come on, you goober heads. This little guy only learnt to read two year'n ago. Hell! He has to put the paper down on the floor to be able to turn the pages. You'ins ain't a-gonna bet that he don't know his baseball? Come on." In truth, he did make book on my baseball knowledge: writing down little bets in his small spiral notebook and collecting ones, fives, and an occasional ten just prior to the monthly challenge. John Quinn, the county commissioner, usually questioned me as he referred to the most recent *Chattanooga Times* sports page for the league leader information. I always knew the answers, and Andrew Ray always won these little bets. Granny eventually found out about this "little game," and, when he escorted me home on the day of his biggest take, she ran Andrew Ray off the porch with her broom.

Aunt Lattie, Andrew Ray's mama, was Granny's oldest sister, owner of the Dixie Diner in Post Oak, and mother of three roust-about sons, two of whom had acquitted themselves well during the war. She and Uncle Sim expected no less. Cousin Andrew Ray had been too young to fight the Japanese or the Wehrmacht, but he was most assuredly draft age by 1956, a status he tried over and over to avoid. Knowing his mother wouldn't help him, he appealed to my grandmother, his doting aunt, to find a way to extricate him from his obligation. She wasn't much help, possessing little understanding of the bureaucratic ways of the Army, local draft boards, recruiting offices, and such. When Granny would sometimes bring up Andrew Ray's plight at the supper table, she gained absolutely no traction with my dad, who didn't care much at all for Andrew Ray and who naturally disliked the boy's efforts to get out of what he *should* do without complaint. I guess this feeling came normally for Dad, who, as a military police-man in Company B of the 794th MP Battalion, had served in the Italian campaign with LT GEN Mark Clark's Fifth Army and had seen horrors he didn't talk about except after he had thrown back a couple of six-packs. Dad didn't stand and salute when Kate Smith sang *God Bless America*, but he was inwardly proud of his service and his country. And we were proud of him. Nope, Andrew Ray wasn't Dad's cup of tea at all. In fact, Dad always said that Andrew Ray was a Deep South version of Eddie Haskell, the conniving and artificially flattering teenager in *Leave It To Beaver* on TV.

As our errant cousin's report date drew near, he tried anything and everything to avoid Army duty. But nothing Andrew Ray tried worked as he sought relief from the Army: not the deeply sympathetic and crocodile-tear pleas to a local state legislator, not the fabricated respiratory issue, not the flat feet ruse, not even the effort to prove temperamental unfitness for military service. He probably would have resorted to Corporal Clinger's donning of corsets, hats, slips, skirts, bras, and frilly blouses to suggest gender confusion (at the time, a possible "out" for a draft dodger), but he knew his brothers would have whipped his ass over that one. Political correctness never abounded in my family. Finally, in the late spring of 1957, Andrew Ray found himself in a basic training company at scenic Ft. Benning, Georgia, and frequently a candidate for KP, extra latrine details, and constant and profane oversight by his grizzled drill instructor. He wanted out in a big way. The breaking point came following the morning he let down his platoon during a practice PT test.

It seems that Andrew Ray feigned a sprained ankle fifteen minutes into a two-mile run. He was taken to the medic's tent, evaluated quickly, and found to be faking it yet again. This time, upon his return to his unit, he was stood at attention in front of his platoon and his butt chewed royally for his slack attitude. But this wasn't all. Far from it. This time his penance was to be shared by his buddies. In the spirit of "one for all and all for one," the entire platoon was required to low crawl back and forth over the asphalt drill pad until almost all the trainees were scratched and bruised and bleeding and unable to sit up. This little activity was designed to incorporate peer pressure into Andrew Ray and his need to adjust his not-so-serious attitude toward basic training. It worked, I reckon. At least it brought things to a head.

That night—after lights out—the muffled sounds of Andrew Ray's screams were heard on both floors of the barracks as his buddies covered him with a blanket and took turns punching him in the gut and the upper arms—hard. Even though a dirty sock had been stuffed partly into his mouth, my cousin's cries could still be heard and were the subject of amusement for his platoon's TAC sergeant, who smiled to hear the shuffling of many feet moving toward the Post Oak boy's bunk. But this old veteran was not about to intervene. He turned over and went back to sleep. The next morning Andrew Ray decided he had had enough.

The weekend following the platoon-size blanket party in the barracks, Andrew Ray high tailed it to Post Oak, Georgia. Somehow he had managed to get off post, rent a car, and mush on up the highway before his absence was detected. He drove straight to his mother's house off Cleburne Street, but Aunt Lattie wouldn't take him in. So Andrew Ray hid his rental car in an abandoned barn, ran the several blocks to our house, knocked furiously on the loose screen door, and was let in by Granny, the compassionate aunt who always took pity.

Ironically, my dad's walking up the driveway following his half-day of Saturday work at Mr. Jaytree's grocery store coincided with the arrival of the olive drab MP sedan in the county jail parking lot across the street. Having seen the MPs, Dad entered briskly through the back door as these two well-honed and crisply starched soldiers strode up the front steps and onto the porch. I suspect that Dad had an inkling that this official visit involved his wife's prodigal kin, Andrew Ray, but my father didn't want to believe it. The MPs were double checking some address information in a notebook as Dad walked into the kitchen. There he found my mom sitting at the yellow Formica kitchen table with a distraught expression on her face and Granny standing near the sink in near desperation. I had been relegated to my room, but I was able to peer out just enough to see and to hear much of the fun. As the knocking began at the front door, Granny's eyes caught my dad's in a quick exchange. She slightly nodded toward the table, covered, as it always was, with a nice, clean, impeccably ironed table cloth that draped almost to the floor. Dad noticed that two folds of the table cloth were barely moving and that a boot toe was slightly emerging from under a chair on the side. His angry gaze quickly shifted back to Granny. She could muster only a pleading, sad, almost tearful response. Her lips silently formed "Please." Dad slumped his shoulders and managed only a disgusted wink. Mom got up quickly to answer the knock. Dad followed her, as did Granny.

The MPs were asked to come into the living room. The one who was a staff sergeant started, "We're sorry for this intrusion, folks, but we're searching for Private Andrew Ray Clark. He went AWOL from Ft. Benning yesterday." He turned toward Granny. "We understand, ma'am, that you're Private Clark's aunt. Is that correct?"

"Yes, that's . . . that's so," muttered Granny, obviously nervous.

"Have any of you seen him in the past eighteen hours or so?" asked the MP.

"No, we haven't, sergeant," Dad said. "Andrew Ray isn't one of our favorite relatives, you know, and I'm not surprised you're after him. I had a feelin' he wouldn't make it through basic. He's in bad trouble, I'll bet."

"Yes, sir, he is," responded the second MP, "and so is anyone who might try to help him. We take AWOL to be a serious offense. Were you in the war, sir?"

"Yes, I was," said Dad. "I was in the 794th MP Battalion for three years. Yep, I was an MP, like you guys."

The NCO continued this line. "Then you'll remember, sir, that AWOL is a bad thing. In time of war, as you know, a soldier could probably be executed for AWOL. You remember?"

"Oh, yeah," agreed Dad, somewhat sullenly. "I remember."

"Then you can give us your word you haven't seen Private Clark?" continued the sergeant.

Dad replied, "No, I don't think any of us would have seen Andrew Ray since he came to Sunday dinner almost four months ago. I really don't cotton to that boy. Can't trust him. I don't even like to break bread with him. He came for dinner that day because I was up in north Chattanooga helping my brother Fletcher fix some furniture." Dad slightly hesitated. "You got any black sheep in your family, sergeant?"

"Do I ever!" The soldier became animated, remembering something he probably didn't wish to remember. "But I need to have some good sour mash bourbon in me in order to talk about family. You know how it is."

"If you fellers weren't on duty, we'd slip on back to the work shed and find some bourbon," Dad agreed cordially.

"I appreciate it," said the MP. "But I guess we'll get on up the road, sir. We know that Private Clark might have a couple of buddies in Westview, Tennessee, just over the state line. Y'all take care, now."

The MPs politely left. We all watched as they got into their car and pulled out into Lafayette Road, no doubt to connect north to Highway 41 and on toward Westview. I had joined my family by this time and observed as Dad groped for the sofa arm to steady himself. Granny placed a hand on his shoulder and said softly, "Thank you, Red. I know you ain't got nothin' for Andrew Ray and that meetin' with them soldiers was hard for you. I . . . I love you for that."

My dad, even with his problems with the bottle, was Granny's favorite son-in-law. He gently patted Granny's hand. "It's OK, Franny," he said. "There's riff-raff on my side of this family, too. But I'm gonna talk with Andrew Ray now, and y'all need to take Mike and maybe walk on over to McEachern's Drug Store for a soda. You understand?"

They did and left. From my overhearing Dad's conversation with Mom a couple of days later, I realized that Dad had pretty much severed any future contact with our wayward cousin. When Dad had walked back into the kitchen after the MPs' departure, a meek, halting voice came from under the table. "They gone, Red? Damn! What 'em I a-gonna do now? Maybe I can stay out yonder in your work shed for a week or so. Then I'll call my buddy in Kentucky and drive on up to see 'em. You don't mind, do you?"

Red Lockhart was around five-eight and weighed close to 150 pounds at the time of Andrew Ray's sojourn under the Formica table. A small man, my dad was solidly built and strong, the result, I'm sure, of years of lifting and throwing quarters of beef over his shoulder and carrying around large boxes of packaged bacon and sausage every day. He had also been trained, as a former MP, in a few physical restraint techniques. As Andrew Ray finished his plea, Dad reached under the table, grabbed one of the scared fellow's legs, and dragged him unceremoniously out into the middle of the kitchen. Then Dad stooped down, placed his right knee firmly into Andrew Ray's chest, and took each side of the deserter's head in those vise-grip, meat cutter's hands. He leaned in close to Andrew Ray's left ear. "Mind? Will I mind? Listen good to me, you worthless SOB. You realize what could'a happened here today? You know what it would'a meant if those MPs had found you here? Did you even think how much trouble we'd all be in? And your Aunt Franny? And little Mike? No, I can tell you that all that mattered to you was YOU!"

"Red, you're a-hurtin' me. Let me get up. We's family, ain't we? Please let me up." Cousin Andrew Ray was wondering whether he would have had a better chance with the MPs.

"Yeah, I'm gonna let you up. Then you're gonna walk out that back door and never, ever come back here. Don't you ever take advantage of Franny's goodness again. She's too good for her own good sometimes. I tried to divert the MPs because of her, not you. But I *ain't* good. And I've got a temper. And if you come back to this house, I'll turn you over in a skinny minute to whatever law officers have come for you. But they won't get you until I've whipped the hog crap outta you first. You understand?" Dad was livid.

"OK. OK. Just let me up." Andrew Ray was in a good bit of pain.

Dad cooled a little and let our cousin up. Andrew Ray was instructed to sneak out the back door, make his way quickly out of our yard and through the dense shrubbery over behind the Masonic Lodge three houses down, and on to Kentucky or wherever. Dad didn't want the MPs to see Private Clark running out the front door if they'd decided to circle back and do a bit of after-the-fact surveillance. Dad said nothing else and simply pointed to the back door.

Somehow, in some circuitous way involving, no doubt, bribery, the calling in of favors, or small-town blackmail, Andrew Ray was able to receive an honorable discharge from the Army without one more day of basic training. In fact, he never saw Ft. Benning again. He was not required to perform any sort of compensatory service. He spent no quality time in the stockade at Ft. Leavenworth. Rumor had it that Stroman E. Wilson, Esq., a Post Oak ambulance-chasing attorney of questionable repute, arranged for Andrew Ray's discharge because Mr. Wilson, Esq., had spent a few festive evenings with Senator Ashworth in Atlanta. Mr. Wilson knew a thing or two about the night life in a seedy area of our capital city way off Peachtree Street—and, if need be, he was more than willing to talk with a reporter for the *Atlanta Journal* about Senator Ashworth's close friendship with a young lady who worked in this area. Senator Ashworth had pulled some strings regarding Andrew Ray. It's not always righteous living that has its rewards, I reckon.

Andrew Ray Clark continued down the tangled path he had established for himself early on. He took up serious gambling and drinking and womanizing and chain smoking. He disliked normal work of any kind and would spend more time and energy trying to avoid honest work than in merely doing the work to start with. And he had opportunities: a counter clerk position in an auto parts store in Post Oak, a rural mail carrier, a used car salesman, a cook in his mama's Dixie Diner. But none of this suited. He later became a close friend of the brother of a successful casino manager from New Jersey. Andrew Ray's own brothers used to say that this good friend was heavily involved in gambling along the East Coast, perhaps dabbling occasionally in "non-refusable offers" from the Bonanno crime family. Later down this convoluted pathway, when Andrew Ray was into his early fifties, he was found dead one afternoon in his apartment just outside the Post Oak town limits. Cause of death was listed as cirrhosis of the liver, but this disease usually doesn't possess symptoms related to ligature marks around the neck, marks that one of the EMS technicians at the scene claimed were there. Out of respect for the family, no one pursued our cousin's suspicious passing.

I've said numerous times that small Southern towns produce numerous eccentric and/or just plain odd and often worthless characters. On one TV episode of *Designing Women* some years back, Julia Sugarbaker said it well, and it went something like this: "In the South, we like our eccentric characters a lot. Why, we even put 'em out on the front porch for everybody to see." I guess Andrew Ray was one of these. But, you know, I can still recall Andrew Ray's grief on the day of my grandmother's funeral in the small Post Oak Methodist Church, now a tacky wedding chapel following the new church's raising on property owned by cousins Maisey and Thornton Turnbuckle. Cousin Andrew Ray cried and cried that day, wailing "Aunt Franny, oh, Aunt Franny, what'll I do?" until the Markson brothers took him outside. His love for Granny wasn't eccentric.

He had his faults, I reckon, but, then, Lord, don't we all?

The Yankee Salesman Comes
to Post Oak—and Leaves

A t just after 5:30 on a balmy, early fall afternoon in 1954, a yankee salesman drove into Post Oak and pulled his Buick diagonally into a parking place in front of the Dixie Diner. These late 1940's and early 1950's Buicks were known for their wide, toothy, chrome grills. My older son, at age eight or so, received braces; when he smiled, the chrome glow sort of had the Buick look. Anyway, the man exited his car, stepped up on the sidewalk, and slid a nickel into the parking meter. I guess you can never be certain of the time a small town will shut down the parking meter shift. This fellow was observed to have on a slightly too tight, wrinkled brown suit with the coat's elbows worn pretty smooth; a dingy once white shirt with the fourth front button and one cuff button missing; a red and yellowish patterned tie maybe three years out of style; and scuffed, two-toned, brown and white wing tips in need of new heels and a good shine. He looked the part.

Now the first thing that might have clued the salesman that this particular afternoon in Post Oak would not turn out in his favor was his abrupt meeting with Up and Down. We'd probably label ol' Up and Down as "homeless" and/or cognitively challenged in the third decade of the 21st century when such labels are necessary to classify all categories of our social strata. I have a close social worker friend who keeps up with all of these professional euphemisms, by the way. Technically,

Up and Down had no specific home address although many said he spent most nights in Mrs. Corley's storage shed. Three or four days a week she'd also run out some leftovers to him along with some iced tea in the summer or hot coffee on nippy late fall and winter mornings. One or two other ladies also made sure that Up and Down was fed most days. The cooks at the Dixie Diner and Chow Place would occasionally provide the downtrodden guy with morning muffins and a mid-day sandwich.

Our cousin, Thornton Turnbuckle, had a rickety, cold-water shower stall behind his ESSO station, and Up and Down was allowed to use this shower when Mrs. Corley would tell him it was time. This strange fellow's shirt, sweater, pants, and shoes were ratty and disheveled, but a number of Post Oakians saw to it two or three times a year that Up and Down was given cast-off clothing items. These gestures got him through. He was always unmatched and sometimes a little mis-sized, but he never went without food and the basic clothing necessities.

His name itself provokes curiosity. In brief, Up and Down walked every day "up and down" Post Oak's main street—called Cleburne Street—from Raeford's Gulf Station on the south end to a street beyond the Chow Place drive-in on the north. Up and down, over and over, day in and day out, walking Cleburne Street, mumbling indistinguishable hellos to folks he'd pass but never able to engage in complete conversation. He'd amble around the gas pumps at Raeford's when he reached that location, sort of wave to Curley Raeford, and begin again the trek toward the Chow Place. Constantly, inexorably in motion, he seemed driven to reach a destination the importance of which no one other than Up and Down knew. You see, Up and Down was certifiably mentally handicapped in a time when the state left the management of such issues pretty much up to the churches, concerned citizenry, and local governments. My granny would say, "Ol' Up and

Down's as crazy as a bessie bug, poor ol' thing." The entomological identity of a bessie bug was never fully understood, but we never questioned Granny about it.

When he'd encounter a person he didn't know, Up and Down would stop and say something that sounded like, "Ahh, ahh . . . err . . . howyoubeen, howyou, howyou?" But it all ran together, and, paired with Up and Down's constant head nods, the effect could be rather unsettling to a stranger. Also, these curious tics, coupled with this fellow's substantial six foot, two inch height and habitual scowl, could become offputting in a hurry to someone not familiar with this denizen of ol' Post Oak. Certainly, Up and Down meant no harm and could even be depended on to lend assistance to Post Oak ladies who dropped grocery bags or to little boys who fell off their bicycles or even to Commissioner Quinn when the need arose to hand out political re-election cards. And this aid was accepted and appreciated with no hint of reluctance or concern or fear. The commissioner was usually glad to give Up and Down a pittance for the campaign work. Obviously, however, yankee salesmen had no institutional memory about Up and Down.

In fact, this particular yankee salesman's long drive down Highway 41 from up near Evansville, Indiana, had been arduous and slow, and he wanted a drink and a filling meal, in that order. He scanned both ends of the sidewalk briefly then straightened his tie and walked toward the front door of the Dixie Diner. It was at that point—three steps from the diner's front door—that he saw Up and Down. The odd fellow began, "Ahh . . . err . . . howyoubeen . . . ?" Combined with his slow movement toward the salesman, this indistinct language appeared to threaten the stranger, who moved a step back and brought both arms up in a kind of defensive posture.

"Get away from me, you idiot!" the yankee almost yelled. "Don't come any closer." He raised his right arm with fist cocked. "Leave me alone. I'll knock the hell outta you!"

Up and Down became quizzical and probably thought this new fellow needed help. "Howyoubeen . . . howyou?" he repeated, moving ever closer to the now frightened salesman. Then, without further thought, the Northerner shoved Up and Down away and muttered something obscene to him. At this point the deficient street person regained his balance, looked down, and slowly walked away, more confused and sad than usual.

The yankee was flustered but regrouped in a hurry. He adjusted his suit coat and entered the diner with the air of one who was accustomed to different restaurants on many different nights; having warded off the threat of the cognitively impaired guy on the street, the yankee now seemed to exude a certain status of superiority. Doubtless he wasn't about to allow the carpetbagger tradition to die from lack of interest in this backward, hayseed town. Only six or seven guests were having supper in the diner at this early hour, and none noticed the man as he occupied a stool at the counter. One other guy was seated three seats further down from the new arrival and was half-heartedly working the crossword puzzle in the day-old *Chattanooga Times*.

Some five years before, my great aunt Lattie's Dixie Diner had opened as a clean, simply appointed restaurant that catered to local clientele who stopped in for meat-and-three plates on days when the eighteen-mile drive to Chattanooga was not convenient. The floor plan included eight square tables for four, six large booths on a side wall, and the counter with eight stools in front. A customer would pay out at the cash register located at the end of this green Formica counter not far from the entry door. Postcards of local Post Oak buildings—both past and present—adorned a rack beside the cash register. A Viewmaster slide device was also on the rack, with a pre-set "See Rock City" slide wheel at the ready. As a kid, I loved the Viewmaster. Groupings of Currier and Ives prints graced the diner's walls with one small bulletin board provided for postings of community events and special programs at Post Oak High School. And behind the cash register was a Bank of Post Oak calendar that also provided the current football schedule with scores for the Post Oak Cougars. The Cougars had split their first four games at this point in the season. It was apparent that the Dixie Diner was a home cooking type of eating place with nothing fancy in the way of décor or menu items. But no one in Post Oak needed fancy; we wanted only a clean, comfortable place to eat and talk with our neighbors when the need arose.

One waitress, Maggie Shelton, was working the counter and cash register when the Northerner came in. Maggie was a single mom in her early thirties, was attractive enough in a rough-hewn kind of way, and could be pleasant—or not—depending on the extent of trouble she had experienced that morning getting her two boys off to school. That particular morning had not gone well: Roddy had spilled his oatmeal onto the recent Frank Yerby novel Maggie kept at the table, and Joey let in the neighbor's dog and allowed the muddy mutt to jump onto the sofa. Maggie was only too glad at last to deposit her kids at school and turn her 1949 Chevy back onto Cleburne Street toward the Dixie Diner.

As the salesman settled in, Maggie was freshening the other counter customer's coffee and beginning to dry a few water glasses next to the Coca-Cola dispenser. When she didn't jump at the chance to see to the salesman's needs, he rather loudly announced, "Hey! What's a guy gotta do to be noticed 'round here? Come on, honey buns, I need a drink. Whatta ya say?"

In addition to the day's grand start with her boys, Maggie had received a call from her lawyer, who told her that her ex-husband's child support—long in arrears—wouldn't be coming in any time soon because ol' Tommy Shelton was in the county work farm in Valdosta for 90 days. Tommy had given one of his South Georgia girlfriends a black eye, and she'd promptly reported his fisticuffs to the local sheriff, who locked Tommy up post haste. Maggie was in no mood to be called "honey buns" on this specific afternoon or on any afternoon in the foreseeable future given her lousy luck with men. She put down her drying towel and walked slowly over to the brusque, impatient yankee. "What'd you say, mister?" she asked with an edge of pissed-offness to the tone.

"I've been on the road all day, honey. I need a vodka tonic with a cut of lime. Smirnoff, if you got it. And move it along, babe." He gave Maggie a knowing wink. The salesman reeked of that worldly self-assurance that comes with too much time spent in too many cheap hotel bars.

"Two things, mister," started Maggie. "One, we ain't got no vodka tonic because this here's a dry county, and, two, I ain't your honey buns or your babe. Now here's the menu with today's specials clipped right chere on the front. I'll be back when you'ins is ready to order."

The yankee was incredulous. "A dry county! A dry county! Dammit if this ain't the hickiest place I've ever seen." Then he let up a bit. "Come on, honey. I'll bet you've stashed a bottle of liquor somewhere in the back of the kitchen, right? Gimme a drink on ice in a regular water glass, your boss won't notice, and I'll order in a few minutes." He had already noticed that Maggie wasn't totally unpleasant to look at, and he was planning to do a little sweet talk to encourage some companionship with her at the first chat and chew motel he could find outside of town. As he suggested the hiding place for the liquor, he took Maggie's left forearm and pulled her over close. She resisted, but his action caught her off balance. She stumbled against the counter closer to the salesman.

Hearing something from the front that didn't sound exactly right, Aunt Lattie emerged from the back of the diner at the time Maggie fell toward the new customer. Now it shouldn't be lost on anyone that at the time Aunt Lattie (actually, my great aunt, but who's counting?) was a stocky, gray-haired, sort of plump-faced woman in her late fifties. She was about five feet ten inches tall and weighed close to 180 pounds. By then a widow, she was a good businesswoman accustomed to taking care of things on her own. Those who remember her well say that she had large hands for a woman and could unload crates of bananas, turnip greens, and cabbage as well as stack bags of Idaho potatoes and oranges. She could stand head to head with even a big man where manual labor was concerned. She took in the scenario involving Maggie and the salesman with a frown and moved toward the ruckus quickly. Maggie struggled back and tried to release the man's grip, but she was having trouble doing so. The man smirked a bit and continued to play with the waitress. He never saw what was coming.

Aunt Lattie had seen and heard enough. She approached without being noticed, grabbed the man by the nape of the neck, and whirled him around on the stool. Those counter stools were good for whirling, you know. And Aunt Lattie had the guy by a good 30-40 pounds. She let go of the back of his neck with her right hand and exchanged neck for tie, almost with one motion. She yanked the yankee forward and off the stool. With her left hand she reached down and took a good, firm hold on his man parts, squeezing as she went. The salesman grunted then let out a mild scream of pain as Aunt Lattie increased the squeeze pressure. "Open the door, Tommie Joe," she said to the black bus-boy cleaning the first booth. He did as he was told.

Aunt Lattie pulled her captive along and out the door, walking backwards as she dragged him with her. He shuffled forward behind her but close, realizing that if he didn't keep in step, a stretching and ripping sensation would add immeasurable discomfort to an already hurtful situation. A few of the local customers had arisen as if to assist the powerful woman, but no one needed to. They settled back to watch the fun. Now the yankee was thrashing around and starting to beg to be released. He was holding the hand around his privates in an effort to lessen the grip. But when he tried to pull her hand off, she tightened up. You could see the excruciating pain in his eyes. "Please, oh, lady, please let go," he gasped. "I'll leave . . . right now . . . and apologize . . . whatever you want me to do. Oh, please!"

Aunt Lattie could tell which car belonged to this outsider, so she pulled him over to a point near the car's grill. Her grip had not tapered off. The Buick's gleaming chrome teeth seemed almost to smile, as if slightly amused at the plight of its smart-alecky owner. "All right," she said, with her lips pursed, "now I'm a-gonna turn you a-loose, you son-of-a-bitch. And when I do, I'll wanna see your damned tail lights movin' south toward Braggtown. Maybe you can find one of them Lorch County gals to treat you nice, and maybe you can find a drink. But not here. I'd better not know that the sun set tonight on your scroungy ass in Post Oak, Georgia."

For good measure, Aunt Lattie gave him one more full squeeze as she released her double grip. The guy screamed again and slumped against the car's hood then slid to the sidewalk. She walked to the front door of the Dixie Diner and looked back. The yankee salesman was groping to find his car keys as he finally managed to get up. He was alternately softly rubbing his genitalia and massaging his neck as he tried to unlock the driver's side door. As could be expected, in his painful, shaking, bewildered state, he promptly dropped his keys, which bounced once and slid behind the left front tire. He lowered himself to almost a squatting position—although his throbbing privates wouldn't allow a full squat—and began reaching for the keys. Try as he might, in his sensitive state he couldn't quite reach them. Out of the corner of his left eye, he could see the large, muscular woman stepping away from the diner and beginning to move back toward him, obviously losing her patience with the slowness of his frantic but unsuccessful effort to escape. Then another hand reached under the car, took the keys out, and held them out gently to the yankee. "Howyoubeen, howyoubeen?" muttered ol' Up and Down, trying to make up for whatever affront he perceived he had caused earlier. The salesman quickly took the precious keys, nodded at the source of help, and with great discomfort gingerly moved into the driver's seat. It didn't take long for him to back out and head south.

Aunt Lattie moved back into the restaurant, winked at Tommie Joe, gently patted Maggie on the back, and looked over at the customers who by then had all gathered at the front window to watch. "Reverend Stoneman and Tippi, Jess and Mary Lou, the rest of you—don't ya'll want a slice of our lemon meringue pie for dessert? It's the house special tonight. It's mighty good. And, Maggie, get ol' Up and Down a piece of that pie and a plastic fork."

I've often wondered what the yankee salesman thought as he drove south toward Atlanta that evening, nursing his pride and badly bruised male jewels, thinking about the crazy guy he couldn't understand, and wondering just how and why it had all happened. I don't even know what he was selling, but I'll bet he never came through Post Oak again.

A Message to Topps Chewing Gum Company ... and to Mom

"Dammit to hell! You stole my Mickey Mantle! You took'em from my shoebox Monday . . . and you're just a shitass and a common thief. I hate you!" I had just publicly accused my best friend, Will Weaver, of committing an heretical, unforgivable act among those of us who collected baseball cards in Post Oak, Georgia, in 1956.

You could play hardball in trade sessions, you could swap your duplicates for good players your trading buddy didn't know enough about to protect, but you could never, *ever* steal a card from a pal. I had also used the term *shitass*, a derogatory, demeaning, almost proper noun reserved for those who had stepped outside the Post Oak kid code in every conceivable way. It's my recollection now that I had learned this word only a few scant weeks before, but what a grand opportunity to demonstrate my developing vocabulary! I had even used this word in front of several of our friends along the third base foul line at the American Legion field. But I knew Weaver had swiped my best card, and, absent a witness or any real proof and living in the pre-DNA era, I could think of nothing to do other than confront him and brand him for what I thought he was. However, with this accusation, I had over-committed and let my temper cloud my judgment, a trait I would carry into adulthood. On that ill-fated day at the Legion Field, I realized that action now must accompany the strong language.

My tirade over, I swung hard on Weaver, surprising him and connecting to the left side of his jaw. He staggered back a bit, and a small trickle of blood oozed from his lower lip. When he didn't fall down, a fall that would have ensured my escape, my whole life flashed vividly before my eyes. You see, Will was big for his age and a damned good fighter. I'd seen him whip a high school guy one day over this fellow's crude remark about Will's older sister, Wanda Jo. Will had lit into this gentleman, Toby Black, oblivious to a couple of well-landed blows by the backpedaling Black and focused only on hurting this guy as much as possible before someone stopped the fight. Will had won hands down. In contrast, in those days I was skinny, wore glasses, and possessed speed but little strength. I also relied more on diplomacy than sheer fighting ability to get me out of trouble. But our friendship notwithstanding, I knew that Weaver was a minute away from plowing into me to exchange blood for blood, and there would be no parity in the exchange. He had to crunch me, of course, because a small crowd of our friends had gathered to watch the fun and Weaver couldn't look bad in front of a bunch of our types.

Even today, over sixty years later, it's almost too painful for me to talk about what happened next. Suffice it to say that my effort to shield myself from Weaver's series of fast-track, sledgehammer blows was quite puny: my scrawny arms provided practically no defense at all. I vaguely recall falling to the ground, covering my face, and feebly punching back as I descended. Rabbit McManus later claimed that Weaver would have still been beating on me way past supper time if ol' man Tater Patterson, who was mowing the outfield grass that day, hadn't run over and pulled Weaver off. "You fellers break it up," Tater said. "I ain't a-gonna call your mamas yet, but, damnation, I sure will if'en y'all don't stop this here fightin'. You'ins hear me?" Weaver slowly let me up.

This fracas could be traced to our ubiquitous baseball card habit, as you can tell, about which more should be said ... a good bit more. We'll come back to the fight, I promise.

My baseball card obsession took off big time during the 1956 season. I was eight years old that year and in the third grade. Oh, I had dabbled a bit with cards the season before—and especially liked the 1955 Bowman color television cards. But a year later Topps Chewing Gum Company bought out Bowman, and the only cards you could get were the larger format (2-5/8" x 3-¾") with a tinted head shot and a vignette of the player in action. The card backs contained the cards' series numbers, vital information of physical traits and hometowns, a few cartoon frames about the players, and the previous year and career statistics. I fell into this hobby hook, line, and sinker and obsessed over my 1956 cards from late March until two or three weeks into the start of school in September. This hobby became ingrained and lasted until I entered the ninth grade at Post Oak High School in 1962. Actually, I collected through the 1962 season, but by that time, most of my buddies had kicked the habit and were on to NASCAR, *Hot Rod Magazine*, bream fishing, freshman basketball, and girls, not necessarily in that order. But my recollection focuses mainly on the 1950s.

For most of us during the 1956-1960 era, a baseball card collection depended on several factors:

1. the acquisition of money to finance the acquisition of cards (As I recall, you could buy cards individually for a penny apiece—with a small slab of bubble gum—or you could lay down a whole nickel for a pack of six cards along with a thicker slab of gum, the preferred method. In both retail modes, the packs provided the wonderfully sweet smell and spread of bubble gum dust the instant the packs were opened.);

2. a source from which to buy your cards (Two drug stores and one small grocery store carried baseball cards in Post Oak in 1956.);

3. a place to store your collection (For me and most of my friends, this site was a sturdy shoebox with a tightly fitting lid. This shoebox usually resided on the floor of the closet in your bedroom.);

4. enough rubber bands to secure your cards organized, not by numbered sequence, but according to team affiliation; and

5. enough close friends or cousins of like age who would enter into serious trading negotiation without trying to cheat you.

These requirements must seem archaic to those who today collect baseball cards by means of eBay auctions, online purchase, sophisticated card grading techniques, and secure storage.

Another collecting principle is important and time specific to the mid-1950s. But we couldn't influence it. A matter entirely out of our control as card collectors had to do with the way in which our suppliers bought and distributed baseball cards in Post Oak, Georgia, during my childhood. Topps printed and wholesaled cards by series back then and not by any sort of random formula. In a small market like Post Oak, the three card sources would buy boxes of the early series cards at the beginning of the baseball season. We'd buy up these cards with gusto—until we had collected almost all of the early series players. Then we stopped buying. With luck, these boxes of early series cards would run out at the same time as our grubby and bubble gum sticky hands had given our dwindling nickels and dimes and quarters to acquire all of these first issue cards.

But it never happened that way. Our suppliers wouldn't order additional boxes, of course, until they had sold the existing inventory. They obviously couldn't sell what we wouldn't buy. And we weren't about to buy cards that would become only more duplicates for our collections. Heck! They didn't know that Topps had a system and that we were on to the system, even if we couldn't give it a name or really describe it. I should admit that this system wasn't always adhered to by the Topps people. One day I acquired a Willie Mays card in a regular pack of low series cards. But this goldmine was a rarity. All in all, we certainly couldn't challenge the purchasing habits of local businessmen, guys who knew your parents well and were probably related to a lot of our moms and dads. This card stalemate continued unless one of us happened to go outside our limited Post Oak market to buy cards or unless we happened across a larger market friend or cousin who had access to the higher series cards. In mid-August of 1956, I was privy to this cousin windfall.

I can't stress enough that baseball card collecting was an expected rite of passage for me and for most of the guys I knew and ran around with. Most of us considered these cards to be a precious part of our burgeoning manhood and a way to offset at least partly our boring Post Oak lives. Now we weren't into the card flipping phenomenon that a lot of kids favored. And while we would occasionally take our cards out and place them on the living room rug by position around an imaginary diamond and then invent a game generally governed by the throw of dice, we never mistreated our cards: wrote on them, folded them, or attached them with clothespins to the spokes of our bicycle wheels (perish forbid!). We'd heard that yankee boys our age would do this sort of thing, but they must have had a constantly replaceable supply of cards. We didn't.

All of this stuff about the hobby—and the art—of card collecting is designed to justify the importance that day of my fight with Weaver. No one in Post Oak had acquired a Mickey Mantle card at that point in the summer, yet I managed to get one. And maybe I did brag a little as I showed off my rare find to my buddies, including, of course, Weaver. Anyway, my

Mantle card had come to me through a resourceful trade with my cousin Wayne, who lived in Dalton, Georgia, a much larger place than Post Oak and located about 13 miles to the south of my fair hometown. Dalton would have had many more outlets for baseball card stockpiles, ergo, the reason for Wayne's possessing a card in a higher series than any cards then available in Post Oak. I think I swapped two Nelson Burbrinks, a Mickey McDermott, a Joe Collins, an Ed Roebuck, and an Andy Seminick for the Mickey Mantle. All of my cards involved in the swap were duplicates and could easily be given up for the Mantle. Truth be known, I would have given up much, much more, maybe even my pet lizard, Ralph!

How I relished my revelation of the Mantle find on the Monday following my weekend acquisition in Dalton. Since it was raining, Will Weaver's front porch happened to be our gathering place on this particular day. I think five of us had assembled there to re-examine our collections. By this time, we were all so familiar with each others' cards that we could predict what we'd see as one of our friends would release the rubber band from, say, his Milwaukee Braves players and sift through to show us his Braves cards along with any new finds. We would sometimes take turns showing our cards in this manner, especially if it'd been a good while since we'd revealed recent acquisitions. When my turn came, I slowly pulled off the rubber band on my New York Yankee team, placed the Yankees team card to one side, and began to peel off the players one by one. I was envied by a number of my buddies because, somehow, I had found a high-numbered Yogi Berra, and Yogi was always the last card in my Yankees team packet. But this time I reached for a card beyond Yogi, carefully placed it face up on the porch beside my shoebox, and leaned back to watch the reactions. Brendon Masters was the first to notice. "Jesus, Lockhart! You've got Mickey Mantle! Lookee here, fellers!

Lockhart's done got a Mantle card! How in the world . . ." He was quickly pushed aside by two other guys.

"OK, Lockhart, how'd you get it?" Weaver was simply amazed and excited. "Didcha get it when y'all went on vacation to Panama City? Did them rich aunts yore always talkin' 'bout up in Chattanooga give you the Mantle? Naw, hell! They wouldn't know about ball cards. But it had to come from someplace other'n Post Oak. Tell us now!"

"Y'all really wanta know, doncha?" I loved the spotlight, even at this tender age. "OK, you know this past weekend when I went to Dalton with Uncle Tom and Aunt Rebecca? Well, I took some cards and ended up tradin' with my cousin Wayne. He's got a pretty good collection, and he must've found some stores in Dalton that sell out boxes way before Dr. McEachern and them other Post Oak places. He's been able to move on to the next couple of series, and Wayne's done got Mantle and Gil Hodges and Whitey Ford and a bunch of other players we ain't seen 'round here. He wanted some of my duplicates, and we hit up a trade. And now I got Mantle!"

Each buddy wanted to hold Mickey for a little while before passing him on. Everyone adhered to the code, though, and there was no rubbing on Mickey with any greasy or bubble gum encrusted fingers, of which there was a gracious supply. Weaver, who was an inveterate Yankee fan, held the card for a long time, gently touching the face, turning the card over to read Mantle's impressive stats, holding the card by the edges, and looking closely almost as if to ensure its authenticity. "I don't s'pose you'd trade him, Lockhart? I'll give you any three of my Dodgers plus my Dodgers team card. That'd include Don Newcombe, y'know." Weaver could strike a hard bargain. He knew the Dodgers were my favorite team, and he was more than willing to part with Newcombe, Duke Snider, even Johnny Podres to be able to insert Mickey Mantle into his Yankee team packet. I suspect he also hoped I'd want to acquire these Dodger players to remind me of the Dodgers' previous year World Series triumph over the Yanks.

"Not a chance, Weaver," I said. "How about Yogi for the trade you wanna make? He's havin' a really good year, y'know?"

"Nope. It's gotta be Mantle." Weaver was adamant and appeared to be already taking too much of a proprietary interest in my sacred card. I didn't like the way he kept holding onto this prized cardboard trophy, sort of possessive-like and maybe threatening. But in a few minutes he reluctantly returned the card, and I carefully placed it back with my other Yankee players, attached the rubber band around the team, and positioned the Yankees toward the bottom of my stacks. Mrs. Weaver came out then and invited us in for a glass of lime Kool-Aide. We moved our shoeboxes back under the porch swing and followed her into the house. In a little while, the rain stopped, and we thanked Weaver's mom and all took off for home.

Three days later I retrieved my shoebox from my closet and began the habitual process of looking through the players for each team, a repetitive exercise that was fascinating for me no matter how many times I'd gone through my players before. (I'm not proud of this, but sometimes I still take out my note-books of 1956 and 1958 cards and repeat this sacred rite. Now, of course, my cards reside in three-ring binders replete with nine-pocket sleeves that hold and protect my cards.) Usually, my 1950s process would be an almost daily ritual, but my Aunt Rebecca had visited us on the day following my unveiling of the Mantle card and had brought me a Revell plastic model of a Sherman tank. The painting and assembly had taken almost three full days, I had proudly completed my tank, and I was eager to return to my card collection.

It was late in the afternoon. I brought out my shoebox and jumped with it onto the foot of my bed. Already having poured a glass of Coke and having unwrapped a pack of crème-filled chocolate cupcakes, I settled in for a fun session with my cards. During these times, I'd also run through my duplicates to figure out my next trade strategy. Earl Jaytree somehow had acquired a Del Crandall and an Eddie Mathews, and I needed both. Little Earl, two years younger than the rest of us, wasn't entirely abreast of the intricacies of card collecting. He'd probably go for my loading him up with several colorful duplicates of common players like Bob Speake, Jerry Coleman, Johnny Kucks, Sandy Amoros, Danny O'Connell, Don Ferrarese, and good ol' Nelson Burbrink (It began to seem that I'd get multiple runs of Jerry Coleman, Danny O'Connell, and Nelson Burbrink every time I bought cards.). The scarcity, for us, of a Crandall or Mathews hadn't yet registered with little Earl. After all, this wasn't cheating, in my mind, if Earl ended up with many more cards than he'd released. Quantity over quality, I reasoned. The matter of ethics is sometimes situational *and* relative. And it's OK for an eight-year-old to rationalize about ethics, too, isn't it?

In my satisfying scan of my 1956 card collection, I usually left the Dodgers and Yankees teams for last. I loved the Dodgers and, while not loving the Yanks, appreciated that team's ongoing dynasty. When I finally took out the packet of Yankee players and flipped through my stash, I gasped and jumped off the bed. Mickey Mantle was AWOL. I scoured my room: under bed sheets, all over the closet floor, all over my small desk, into shoes. I shook shirts and jeans and felt through all pockets. I took out all my games, Lincoln Logs, and Ft. Apache set and carefully searched every nook and cranny of every box involved. My Mantle card was nowhere to be seen. I even resorted to asking Mom and Granny for help, but it was all to no avail. That evening I was beyond solace and slept very little.

It's time now to backtrack to the 20 minutes or so prior to my fight with Weaver at the Legion Field. Right after choosing up sides, Weaver gathered us near third base. In a somewhat cocky way, I thought, he showed all of us his "new" Mickey Mantle card and told us he had gotten it in a pack of cards his dad had bought for him in Atlanta. No way, I quickly concluded. Even Mullet Kinlaw and Froggie Roundbottom seemed doubtful. We argued back and forth about the coincidental nature of Mickey's miraculous appearance at the exact moment of my Dalton trade and subsequent loss of my prized card. Weaver maintained that things like that happened and that I shouldn't attack his good fortune. Then my accusation and surprise punch, followed by my butt whipping. Thank God for Tater Patterson that day!

Bottom line, I couldn't prove Weaver's theft. For days and days after the loss of Mickey and the fight, I moped around the house, seldom went out to play ball with my friends, and lost interest in my Lionel train and even my baseball cards. This wasn't like me, of course, but it was probably a natural reaction. Mom and Dad spent more time with me during those weeks after the fight. Mom took me to the Camera and Craft Hobby Shop in Westview, Tennessee, about eight miles north of Post Oak and bought two model World War II planes for me—even exceeding my weekly allowance by a couple of dollars. And I didn't have to ask for these planes. She also demonstrated an odd interest in my ball cards, leaving my room one night with a couple of empty card wrappers in hand. I didn't think about it much. Later Weaver sort of tried to make up, even apologizing for blacking my left eye and bruising my arms. But he never owned up to involvement in my missing Mickey Mantle. I decided that my life would be complete without Weaver's friendship, so I pretty much avoided him on the ball field and into the first week of the new school year.

I'm convinced that family lives such as the ones televised on *Leave It to Beaver, Andy Griffith, Little House on the Prairie, Father Knows Best,* or *The Waltons* seldom play out in the real world. It's all too melodramatic, too predictable, too goody-goody, too sentimental. Motivation and character reaction are often misaligned. In reality, parents mean well, usually, but they often don't quite know how to interact with their kids at times of kid need, and they misjudge appropriate forms of praise and/or punishment. Mine were often like this. But sometimes they do lay down the necessary bunt, make the good throw from third to first, get the crucial hit with two outs and two runners in scoring position (After all, this *is* a story involving baseball.). On a day three weeks or so following my fight with Weaver, Mom knocked in both runs.

When she came home from work in the tax assessor's office in the court house on that special day, she went to the kitchen for her obligatory cup of coffee, took an envelope out of her purse, and walked to my room. "Honey, somethin' came in the mail today, and I thought you'd want to see it. Maybe it'll make you feel better." She handed me the previously opened envelope.

I paid practically no attention to the return address on the envelope in my effort to get inside. If I'd been a bit more diligent, my excitement would've increased. The address read "Topps Chewing Gum Company, 254 36th St., Brooklyn, New York." No zip code appeared; we didn't have zip codes then. In my haste to unravel the mystery, I turned the envelope upside down, causing the main item to fall to the floor. Landing face up at my feet, the image of the same smiling Mickey Mantle I had once owned peered up at me. He almost seemed to be winking. I reached down and gently picked up the card, with special care not to bend the corners. "Gosh, Mom! Where . . . how . . . when did this come? How did you do this?" In my thrill and amazement, I forgot to thank her, so I stepped over to give her a big hug. She patted my head and began her brief explanation.

"When you lost your first Mickey Mantle, I thought about this situation for a long time. I talked to your dad about it. Whether Will stole the card or not, it all didn't seem fair to me. You'd collected cards all summer hoping to get Mickey, and you never did. This Topps company had sorta roped you fellas in, got y'all hooked and eager to keep buying their product. I thought maybe if I wrote to them, explained your collecting all summer and disappointment, enclosed at least a quarter, that maybe they'd send you the Mantle card. We had nothin' to lose, did we? I found the company's address on one of your baseball card wrappers. Anyway, one of the vice presidents sent you the card along with the nicest letter. I feel good about this now. This Mickey Mantle's sorta special. I hope you'll hold onto it."

Even though Mom later threw out two Topps albums and a shoebox full of my baseball cards during an unfortunate family move to Dallas, Texas, in 1959, I managed to keep my 1956 and 1958 sets and a few other cards. By the way, this urban legend about moms throwing out their kids' baseball cards *isn't* a legend: it happened to me and several of my buddies. But I still have the 1956 Mantle and was able, somehow, to finish out a complete set of these cards. They're important to me.

During the sorting out of Mom's belongings following her death in December of 1988, I found the letter from Topps Chewing Gum Company transmitting the Mantle card. The letter was quite brief, but it conveyed a kind, empathetic tone and implied also that Topps was returning Mom's quarter. The vice president, a Mr. Stoner, I believe, thanked my mother politely for her and her son's interest in Topps baseball cards and indicated that he was pleased to be able to comply with her request. He made it clear, however, that this sort of special provision was not something Topps often responded to, but Mom's clarity, obvious love for me, and good writing skill had carried the day. Much later I read an article on the manufacture and distribution of Topps baseball cards, and I realized that Mr. Stoner no doubt interrupted a press run and cut into a large sheet of cards to retrieve the Mickey Mantle. He didn't have to do any of that. Maybe Mom's letter found him on a good day; whatever the case, Mr. Stoner's kindness has restored my faith in industrial America. I remember Mr. Stoner and Topps when the tired and crusty customer service clerk at Wal-Mart lends a deaf ear to my efforts to explain a faulty switch on my new coffee maker. And as an adult card collector when companies like Fleer and Donruss entered the card market in the early 1980's, I remained loyal to Topps.

You know, Mom didn't have to write to Topps either about my Mickey obsession. I doubt this sort of thing is to be found in any Mom job description related to any little junior butthole like me. You must love a kid a lot to do what she did.

I love you, too, Mom. But if, perchance, you happen across those two albums and shoebox of cards in heaven, I'd really like to have them back. There's a great 1957 Hank Aaron in that shoebox.

The Grandmother and the Frog

"Good God a'Mighty!" my grandmother screeched. "It's one of them filthy ol' whiskey stills again! I bet it belongs to that Roundbottom trash, and I bet the Sheriff brought it in when he put ol' Seth Roundbottom back in jail. Why don't they send that worthless ol' man to that big fed'ral place in Atlanta?" On this day in the summer of 1957, we lived in one of a number of rental houses we occupied during my childhood in Post Oak, Georgia. This recently reconditioned home, located across the street from the county jail and the jail's gravel parking lot, afforded us, especially Granny, an unobstructed view of the goings-on at our dilapidated house of detention. She always took full advantage.

Granny had to interrupt her tirade to catch her breath. It wasn't her first such outburst on the subject, but it might have rivaled the louder one a year earlier when she stomped her feet for effect and stubbed her toe in the process. The still's arrival, plus the toe pain, then had elevated Granny almost to the level of conniption, but she managed to keep it at hissy fit mode. Even so, this time she made her commitment known. "Well, I'll tell you one thing," she continued. "My precious little angel and his little friends ain't a-gonna play aroun' that sinful thing! I'm a-callin' Sheriff Samuels right this minute!"

Small Southern towns nurture strange connections. Post Oak, Georgia, in 1957 was no exception. To wit, you'd never imagine that the son of that reprobate Seth Roundbottom and my righteous, church-going, seventy-six-year-old grandmother would ever develop a meaningful relationship. But they did.

Ol' man Seth Roundbottom and his son, Froggie, lived in a rickety shack about three miles east of Rising Buck, an area of Landsford County not known for its refined citizenry. Mrs. Roundbottom had taken off toward Alabama with the three daughters about five years prior to this most recent incident of Granny's loud unrest. Seth and Froggie were left to fend for themselves. Seth and others of his bloodline had migrated to our county in the late 1800s from south Alabama and had tried to establish themselves in farming in a Snopesian kind of way. There might have been twelve-fifteen men in a group that included skanky women and scroungy children arrayed in not-so-well-defined relationships with the men. And these relationships were subject to change with little notice. These people were all dirty, stinky, deceiving, conniving, dishonest, lazy, and often violent. Four of the men, including Seth, had once joined up with the KKK, but even the Klan didn't want them. Think about that. No one around Post Oak wished to interact with them at all, so, by the mid-1950s, Seth and Froggie were the last of the Roundbottom line anywhere around. When share cropping didn't work out for Seth— mainly because no respectable farmer in the county would do business with a Roundbottom—Froggie's dad turned to the only other line of work he knew: the production of untaxed moonshine whiskey.

On the day of Granny's outrage, Seth had indeed just become a guest of the county for another thirty-day stint during which time Froggie was brought in to stay with Mr. and Mrs. Strawbridge, the jailors. Froggie went to school in the morning, ran around with us in the afternoons, and slept in the food and equipment storage room on the jail's first floor at night. Mrs. Strawbridge saw to it that the Frog was given supper almost every evening by reallocating the servings of the meals provided by law to the county's rent-free guests. She insisted also on two baths each week, probably a good thing for all concerned. Her husband would've raised hell at this practice of feeding and bathing the son of an imprisoned Roundbottom, but all of this happened way before the county or state could afford a resourced social services agency, and, well, most folks seemed to like Froggie and even feel sorry for him. Mr. Strawbridge didn't like the situation at all, but he put up with it. Sheriff Samuels cast a blind eye to the whole thing, content to show off his recently confiscated whiskey still and add an inmate to the jail census.

Froggie Roundbottom was the kind of guy you remember as you reflect on your childhood. When his dad was jailed this time, Froggie was in my fourth grade class although the Frog, at eleven, was a full two years older than the rest of us. He was a lean, sinewy fellow who was bigger than we were—because of the age differential—but he never used his size to intimidate any of us or to get his way during any classroom group learning activities. He possessed the kind of ruddy, rough but good-natured face that showed promise of a handsome young man somewhere in the future, but the Frog didn't have much of a positive future, as you can tell.

Frog came to school wearing versions of the same two shirts and one pair of jeans throughout the year. He wore old, scruffed-up tennis shoes, probably Keds, but the brand patch had long since worn off, sometimes with one of the rubber soles flapping when he walked and often with a shoelace missing. His socks were always mismatched. How he played ball so well while coping with these personal clothing flaws was never understood. During the winter, Froggie also wore a torn, dirty, stained, bedraggled gray sweater, never a coat, and seemed to struggle with a perpetual cold. Sneezes and runny noses were all too common for most of us, so no one really noticed that the Frog didn't appear to have breaks in his streak of colds. A cold was just part of his make-up, no matter the time of year.

A trait I've never forgotten was the fact that Froggie was ambidextrous and not the trait that created the Mickey Mantle or Bernie Williams kind of switch-hitting prowess. No. Froggie was completely adept with either hand and either foot, too, I reckon, but we didn't know anything about soccer then and wouldn't have been able to tell if Froggie were equally as good a kicker right-footed or left-footed. Most of the rest of us had dads or uncles who had taught us to play baseball, but poor ol' Froggie had Seth Roundbottom, whose athletic interests didn't move much beyond kicking their mangy old mixed-breed hound or tossing empty beer bottles out into the yard or half-pint whiskey bottles or mason jars against the kitchen stove when the last drops were drained. But somehow Froggie acquired baseball skill.

An important advantage of Froggie's left and right dexterity was his ability to borrow either left-handed or right-handed ball gloves when his team was in the field, depending on his opponents' willingness to allow a Roundbottom to touch any-thing they owned. Froggie was a quick, coordinated ball player who could hit a baseball a long way and catch anything that came even remotely near him. We appreciated his talents as a ball player and always selected the Frog first when we "chose up" for pick-up games after school. Froggie's being two years older than the rest of us was not an issue.

Occasionally I would think about Froggie when it started to get dark and our game would break up. Most of us were lucky: not basking in luxury, we still headed home to warm houses with TV's and comfortable beds and parents and grandmothers who loved us and good suppers and standards for hygiene and homework we hated at the time but deep down appreciated. Froggie went home to Seth Roundbottom and little to eat and a cold, dirty shack and a decrepit cot for a bed and an old Emerson radio that worked when Seth could pay the electric bill and being constantly cussed out for no reason and no parental interest in school work or brushing teeth. The Frog was better off, I guess, at those times when he was allowed to live with the Strawbridges on the first floor of the jail.

My grandmother, Franny Millwood, was "a real corker," as the old folks around Post Oak used to say. She was a strong-willed woman whose love for her family and friends and for her Lord and Savior, Jesus Christ, was legend. Although a Methodist and definitely not a Baptist, she was pretty damned good at sniffing out sin and corruption, and she could be a bit too judgmental about people at times—traits we usually associated with our Baptist brethren and sisthren. At church she sang in the choir, helped with the altar guild, organized and prepared food for the many Methodist covered-dish luncheons, and chaired the local Woman's Christian Temperance Union chapter. If our church had given a Most Valuable Player award in the mid-1950s, Granny would have been a choice candidate.

During the first ten years of my life—when Granny lived with us—I full well knew that she always cared for me and worried about me; she always had my back in any dispute with my friends or with Mom; she would spoil me with extra baseball cards and ice cream whenever the occasion arose; yet she had no compunction about switching my skinny little butt when I screwed up. And even this was OK. You need some structure and some constants and some ground rules when you're a kid, and Granny provided copious amounts of all of this stuff. The hickory switch was just value added.

The connection between Froggie Roundbottom and Granny took place because Froggie was my friend and one of my after-school colleagues when ol' Seth was a guest of the county. Granny never liked it that I would deign to hang around with "that dirty Roundbottom boy," but she tolerated it as long as the Frog didn't come inside the house. But one day a couple of those coincidences of life arose that changed everything.

It started out as a nice, clear, almost warm kind of day in early October. Around twelve of us had gathered in the field near Frampton's Dairy for a game of tackle football. Playing touch was considered a wussy thing to do in Post Oak in 1957. Even so, there was sort of an unwritten agreement that hard tackles, head butting, shirt ripping, and piling on were *verboten*. This day promised to be even more special because Doc Jaytree, who ran a small grocery store across the street from the field, walked over to play quarterback for both sides. Some twenty years before, Doc had been a decent tailback for the Post Oak High School Cougars. Sensing his nostalgia for past football glory, Doc's wife minded the store when he would amble over to direct our offenses, stained apron and all. Doc was the only player for whom touch rules were inserted.

The best thing about this game on this day, without doubt, was that two of our black friends showed up to play, too, and these guys were really good. Segregation was much the order of the day in mid-fifties Post Oak, so our parents would've probably busted us if they had known that we were sometimes integrating our after school games. Now the black grammar school kids attended a small, ill-equipped facility in the "colored" section of Post Oak. But the black high school kids were made to ride a school bus almost twenty miles from Post Oak and back every day to attend a multi-county high school for Negroes in our "progressive," separate-but-equal society. It all made no sense—even in 1957. And, yes, you'll notice that this segregation practice was still in effect over three years following the landmark *Brown vs. Board of Education* case in 1954. Whatever the situation, these games with the black guys probably contributed some years later to the peaceful, non-disruptive integration of Post Oak High School during my senior year. The arrival of the local blacks—all twelve of them—at our school seemed not to be a sudden, forced, cold turkey experience. Heck, it wasn't! We already knew these kids, even if our parents weren't aware of it. As I think back, I would imagine that some of our parents and other Post Oakians resented this absence of struggle and violence. Without a thought to the effects of bigotry and fighting on their youth, these upstanding adults had looked forward to anger and racial division so that an "I told you so" response could be directed toward an intrusive federal government. All of this notwithstanding, we knew when to keep our mouths shut.

The game started well. My team moved quickly to the lead when Doc hit Derrick Lumpkin, the older black boy, with a long TD pass following a fake screen. We had pretty sophisticated plays back then, diagrammed carefully and clearly with Doc's right index finger on the palm of his greasy left hand. Thinking back, I recall how much we enjoyed the huddles with Doc Jaytree: in close quarters, he always smelled like a combination of sliced baloney, sardines, and Vienna (pronounced "Vi-eennee" in Post Oak) sausage. Owners of small-town grocery stores used to smell like this, I reckon.

On the first play after we kicked off, the heavens opened, and an unexpected downpour sent us all scurrying home. Somehow, Froggie ended up with me in our living room. Granny was watching *The Edge of Night* or *The Corners of Day* or some such artfully entitled soap opera on TV, so I don't think she saw the Frog and me slide quietly back toward my room. She would have raised holy hell to see Roundbottom trash in her house. My plastic U.S. cavalry troops were busy defending Ft. Apache from marauding Indians on the floor, a scene of vicious fighting I had left in place from the night before. I went over to my desk to check my homework; I didn't notice that Froggie was transfixed on the battle below. "Frog, I'm gonna read some social studies stuff right now," I remember saying. "You play with the fort or my planes over there or read a couple of my funny books, OK?" As I sat down at my desk to study, I didn't really notice what Froggie had decided to do. What I did notice—and abruptly, too—was that the rain had stopped and the sun had mostly come back out and was shining through my bedroom window.

"Come on, Roundbottom!" I yelled. "The guys'll be back over at the dairy field for the game. Come on!" The social studies assignment be damned. The game's back on, I realized. And the now soppy field would add to the fun of losing footage and sliding and tackling. I ran out of the house, assuming, I guess, that Froggie was right behind me. He wasn't.

Most of the players from the original teams returned to the field, and we played for another hour. My team won, I think, mainly because we had Derrick Lumpkin and Doc Jaytree deemed it wise to continue to throw to him on short routes, down-and-out patterns, and even the "I'll throw it as far as I can and you run under it" design. No one really noticed that the Frog wasn't with us. The third time Lumpkin caught a long pass, Mr. Frampton and John Quinn, the county commissioner, watched it from near the first gas pump at Jaytree's Grocery. They didn't seem too pleased, but no one walked over to say anything to us. I didn't realize it then, but these pillars of the community were witnessing first hand a threat to our all-white social system. I noticed that they counseled Doc Jaytree with serious expressions on their faces when the game was over. Doc appeared sad, even forlorn, as he went back into his store.

When I walked back through the front door of our house, I noticed the TV was off and Granny wasn't around. I could smell something good from the kitchen—beef stew simmering on the stove, I believe. But no Granny. Then I heard muffled conversation coming from my bedroom. As I walked quickly down the hall, I thought I could hear Froggy's voice with the occasional rhetorical grunt of assent coming from an adult female companion. I peeked through the slightly ajar door to see Granny sitting on the edge of my bed in conversation with the Frog, who was down on the floor moving cavalry troops to defensive positions behind the stockade section of Ft. Apache. My room's configuration enabled me to watch this little vignette without being seen myself. Froggy asked, "Mrs. Millwood, does Lockhart—uh, I mean—does Michael have a lot of stuff like this here fort set with all them sojers and Injuns and horses? And them planes over thar. He built 'em, didn't he? Did his paw help 'em with that? And that pile of funny books. And that checker set. Damn! . . . sorry, I mean doggone!" Granny's brow furrowed a bit with the Frog's expletive, and she slightly readjusted the small wad of snuff under her lower lip. Froggie noticed but went on, "Mike's lucky, ain't he, to have all this? And he always gets a new ball glove at the beginning of the season . . . and a bike that he doubles me on . . . and he always has extry pencils he can give me at school. Y'all must be rich, ain'cha?"

"No, Froggie. We ain't rich," said Granny. "But we're lucky to have what we need and to give Mike most of what he wants most of the time. Does your paw give you nice things for Christmas? I hope so." She was sincere in her concern for this downtrodden boy. "And what's your real name? Don't you get tired of bein' called 'Froggie' all the time?"

"No'm," replied the Frog as he tipped over two soldiers towards what I imagined was deadly gunfire or arrows from the Indians. Now that I think about it, the Indians won most of these fights when Froggie was in charge. I reckon he always favored the underdog—or hated uniformed government authority. Picked up this attitude from his father, I'll bet. Froggie continued, "We ain't had Christmas at our place since Maw and the gals took off for Alabammy. That's been near on to five year'n ago now. And I don't reckon Paw cares much about when Christmas is. He don't never say nothin' 'bout it. Hell, it don't matter none. And I ain't never had no name 'ceptin 'Froggie.' Mama started callin' me that when she done noticed that I useta draw them big-mouthed green frogs on 'most everthin' I could get my hands on, like the famly pages in our Bible, old calendars, books from school, and one time I drew a frog on one of Paw's court papers. He tanned me good fer that'un. I don't need nothin' else 'cept 'Froggie.'"

"Hmm," responded Granny. "Froggie, I hope we can become friends and spend some time together. Would you like that? It wouldn't embarrass you none, would it? I mean, your friends wouldn't make fun of you, would they?"

"No'm," quickly answered Froggie. "I ain't got many real friends—'ceptin' Mike and maybe Will Weaver and Peter Tom Robertson. The other fellers at school like me durin' ball games 'cause I'm pretty damned good, but they'd never take me home with'em like Mike does. I'd like to visit with you, iffen you don't mind."

Granny's brow had furrowed again, and this time she removed the snuff on a couple of Kleenexes and prepared to throw the messy concoction away. It was a big deal that she took out her snuff in front of the Frog. She was always private about snuff insertion and extraction, even around me. "Froggie," she gently replied, "I'll look forward to our visits. But you've gotta work on somethin' for me: you've gotta quit usin' cuss words. That kind of language ain't a-gonna get you nowhere in life, and it's 'specially bad to cuss 'round a lady. You understand? I ain't a-fussin', but I want you to try to stop it. It's become a habit—a bad one. And you need to stop it."

"Yes'm," the Frog seemed downcast. "I'll shore try. But it's sorta gotten to the point where my paw 'spects it of me. Cussin' is 'bout the onliest thing he's ever really taught me. He's proud when I lite out with a whole string of bad words, like maybe when I say that stuff, it gives us Roundbottoms 'bout the onliest thing we's known fer. And it's damned—oops, I mean doggone—hard to change my way of talkin' 'tween home and school and out 'round Post Oak. I'm sorry. I'll shore try to stop."

Granny smiled and said, "Good, Froggie. That's 'bout all I can ask for. Tell you what, if you come by here, say, twice a week, and we have our talks, I'll give you a nickel for each visit when you don't cuss. I'll have a jar at the end of my dresser as the reward jar for not cussin'. " She was proud of this strategy, aimed, as it was, to improve the outcast boy's social graces. "If you cuss, though, you haveta give me a nickel back. At the end of the month I'll give you whatever's in the jar. All right?"

"A whole nickel—jest for not cussin'?" Froggie was amazed. "Yes'm, I'll shore do my best. I shore will. Thankee, Mrs. Millwood."

"Good. We've got us a deal then," said Granny. She smiled then continued, "Froggie, do Mr. and Mrs. Strawbridge over at the jail treat you all right? Ever year you seem to spend a lot of time with 'em. I hear they're pretty good folks, but they don't come out much from that jailhouse. Ethel Partin and I—we've talked right much 'bout them and 'bout your situation over there. Do they treat you all right?"

"Yes'm, pretty much, I reckon. They ain't obliged to look out fer me. Mrs. Strawbridge, she feeds me as much as she can from what the county gives 'em for the pris'ners. The ol' man don't complain 'bout me too much. And my sleepin' place is usually purty warm. They gimme an old blanket and some ol' feed bags with straw for pillers. It's OK. And I do some chores for 'em sometimes, even without bein' told. It's OK."

Froggie never ever talked about himself—to anybody. Yet the boy was opening up to Granny. And this was the same woman who insisted that I never bring that Roundbottom trash into the house. At age nine, I had trouble processing these paradigm shifts. But I listened intently at the door as the conversation continued. When I could tell that things were winding down, I eased open the door and walked into my room.

"Hey, Frog, you missed a good game," I said. "You should'a seen Lumpkin on those long passes. Whatcha been doin' in here?" I pretty much knew that he'd been messing around with my cavalry set and talking with Granny, and, to tell the truth, I was fascinated by this turn of events and didn't mind his presence at all.

Granny seemed a little embarrassed and got up quickly to return to the kitchen. As she left, she looked back at us and said, "Mike, it's gettin' close to supper time. Ask Froggie if he wants to eat with us tonite." It used to intrigue me that the women in my family would defer questions to me regarding my friends—when these friends were present in the room and within earshot. It was as if this second layer of communication were somehow necessary and appropriate and more formal. Anyway, Froggie didn't accept the invitation but thanked Granny in the best way he knew how. He then attempted to set my Ft. Apache scenario back up in its previous position and seemed worried that he couldn't remember where all the soldiers and Indians belonged.

"Don't worry about it, Frog," I said. "I need to put all of this stuff back in the closet anyway." I decided not to begin that process and open the closet with Froggie standing there. He didn't need to see the boxes of toys and games and model planes I was fortunate to own. I walked with him to the front door and watched as he plodded, head down, over to the jail. With his arms hanging out his barred cell window that gave him a view of our house, Seth saw where the Frog had been and cussed at him for bothering people.

Granny had watched, too, and said after a minute, "Honey, you want me to help you put up your soldiers now? I know where they go. I'll bet you're tired after all that football."

"No, Granny," I replied tersely. "It's my job to keep my room neat, and I'll do it. Mom 'spects me to. And you agreed not to call me 'honey' or 'precious angel' or any of them other little boy names. I want you to practice not doin' that, OK?"

Have you ever wanted to reach back in time and retrieve something hateful you might have said? When I looked up at Granny after my nine-year-old reprimand, I realized I'd stepped too far. The hurt was clearly there, already forming in her eyes, at the corners of her mouth, and heard even in the heavy sigh.

"Why, certainly I understand, Mike," she said. "Certainly. You're big now, and you can take care of your own chores. I was only a-tryin' to help . . . to help," her words softly drifting off to join the hurt. She turned and walked slowly back toward the kitchen. To this day, I don't understand why I chose that moment to scold the good woman who loved me and took care of me and needed me in her life.

That afternoon's *tete-a-tete* involving Granny and the Frog was to play itself out several times over the next few months. In whatever way he could, Froggie would work it out to end up at my house after school most days. And, for some inexplicable reason, Granny wouldn't need to watch the soap opera she'd been watching forever or even to review her daily devotional in *The Upper Room*. Heck, she'd been tuning in to this soap opera when it was broadcast only on radio. Somehow, if Froggie came by the house, her whole life changed. She welcomed Froggie in, ushered me out to play ball with my friends, and then moved into my bedroom to ensure that the Frog had access to my best stuff.

When Ft. Apache became a little boring, Granny found other items that Froggie might want to explore. One day the two of them were trying to figure out how to assemble a plastic Revell B-25 Mitchell bomber I had bought with my most recent stash: at least four weeks' worth of saved allowance money.

Froggie wouldn't have begun to understand this concept of an allowance from your parents. Anyway, the B-25 assembly had started well. Following the directions closely, I had already painted the barrels of the machine guns and landing tires black, the faces of the pilot and crew with a light flesh-tone (At that time, it hadn't occurred to the Revell big-wigs that "flesh-tone" need not always be a light beige.), and the inner wheels and struts on the landing gear a shiny silver. This work had been tedious, but it didn't matter. Granny decided that Froggie needed to finish this assembly—from the unfolding of the instructions to the layout of all the plastic parts to the collection of the glue and any necessary Testor's paint and my favorite Exacto knife to the precise decisions about where the decals would go. I had been summarily removed from this project—and it was *my* damned model plane financed with *my* money. But it was OK.

On the day of the B-25 assembly, I came home a little early from the ball game. When I walked into the house through the kitchen door, I sensed that something was not quite right. No Granny in the kitchen. No aroma of supper on the stove. No hustle and bustle over near the washer and dryer. All right, I thought, maybe Granny's coffee club at Dr. McEachern's drug store had uncovered some really juicy scoop regarding Reverend Maynard's oldest daughter or maybe James Robert Huskey had broken into Wilbert's Hardware Store again or maybe Ruby Trendle had been asked to step down from her solo soprano role in the Methodist Church choir. You need time to process these kinds of things. But as I stood just outside the dining room door, I heard something. It couldn't be mistaken. It was Granny's voice, and she was giving encouragement—gently—to someone about something obviously important.

I tiptoed to my bedroom and looked in. There they were. Granny was standing over the Frog, who was sitting at my desk. Their being together was no surprise, but this time they seemed more intense. She held the instruction sheet in her right hand with the Exacto knife at the ready in her left hand, and she was pointing to a part that was still attached to a plastic tree, the kind of tree that back then held almost all of the components of all of our model planes and tanks and cars. These plastic trees were ubiquitous. As I watched, she handed Frog the knife and nodded assuredly as he cut and carefully separated two parts from the olive drab tree. Then he spread glue onto one of the parts, the flange on the right wing, and carefully positioned this piece into the proper slot on the side of the fuselage. He slowly replicated this procedure with the left wing. He was a better glue applier than I ever was. Much of the time I was too glue aggressive, so small glue blobs would ooze out from whatever joined assembly I was working on. With Frog, the fit was just right with no excess. I watched with amazement as Frog looked up at Granny and smiled. Come to think of it, I had never seen the Frog smile. She patted him on the shoulder and returned her attention to the instruction sheet.

I must have made a noise of some sort at this point. They both turned to confront me, somewhat embarrassingly, I thought. I broke an awkward silence. "Whatcha doin', Frog?" I asked.

Granny spoke first. "Nothin's wrong here, honey . . . uh, Mike," she started. "I told Froggie he could work on your plane. If it's messed up at all, I'll get you 'nother'un when my Social Security check comes in. He ain't ever had one of these before, and I thought he might enjoy puttin' it together . . . and readin' and followin' the directions . . . and not bein' yelled at. Don't be mad."

"Heck, Granny, I ain't mad," I said. "I never knew you paid much 'tention to me when I was puttin' together my model planes. You know how to do it. Now you and Frog have almost got this sucker put together. By yourselves. And it looks pretty good." I was excited and continued, "OK, don't screw up the decals. Follow the instructions, and don't take the decals out of the water before they're ready. They won't slip off the sheets if they ain't ready, and it's easy to tear 'em apart. I'll get you a glass with some lukewarm water in it. Y'all will do fine." I found myself amazed at the paradoxical scene playing out before me.

I left the room and went to the front part of the house toward the kitchen to get the water for the decals. Mom had come home from work by this time and had also gone to the kitchen to pour herself a cup of several-hours-old coffee.

"Hey, Mom," I said. "Did you have a good day today?"

"Yes, I did," she replied. "Where's your grandmother? I need to ask her about all of us goin' over to Aunt Lattie's this Sunday."

"She's in my room with Froggie Roundbottom," I answered. "But let 'em be for a while. They're about to finish makin' my B-25 bomber. It's great!"

Mom looked a bit incredulous. "With Froggie?" she asked. "Again? They've become good buddies lately, haven't they? He's been over here ever day this week. And playin' with your models. You don't mind that?"

"Nah," I said. "Roundbottom ain't got much to play with. Granny's been helpin' him read the instructions, and I think he's able to follow 'long. This is OK." After a brief reflection, I asked, "Mom, you 'member how Granny used to despise all the Roundbottom folks? Now she spends lotsa time with Froggie. What's changed?"

"Nothin', really," Mom said. "Your granny's realizin' that you're gettin' older and won't need her as much. She needs to be needed. Several things probably goin' on here, honey. Froggie's pitiful, in many ways." She sat down, sipped her coffee, and looked intently at me before saying, "We all need someone to care about what we do. You've got all of us. Your granny knows that Froggie doesn't really have anyone. She probably wants to help him as much as she can."

"Mom, what's a-gonna happen to Froggie?" I asked. "I mean, when he gets a lot older and his dad's sent to jail for a long time . . . and he can't find his mom in Alabama . . . and the Strawbridges don't really care nothin' 'bout him . . . and there ain't nobody else? What'll happen?"

"I don't know, honey," Mom said. "But right now, he's got your grandmother. Let's go see if they've finished your plane."

Froggie and Franny Millwood had indeed finished the B-25, all but the decals. Except for one dribble of glue on the bottom gun turret (my earlier dribble, not Froggie's) and the slightly askew co-pilot, the bomber was in good shape. And this unlikely twosome collaborated on a number of other ventures over the next few months. Granny taught Froggie to play Authors and Old Maids. She helped him with his reading and managed to bring him up to grade level in a short period of time. Our fourth grade teacher, Mrs. Cornwell, couldn't even do that.

Froggie also helped Granny several times in the kitchen as she baked cakes and breaded fish and rolled fryers in corn meal and prepared string beans and creamed corn for supper. Now don't misunderstand. The Frog still played ball with us on many afternoons, but he always found time to be around Granny, too. On occasion, she could convince Froggie to stay and eat supper with us, but he usually went back to the jail or hitchhiked out to the Roundbottom shack beyond Rising Buck. And ol' Frog cut down on his cussing, at least when he was with Granny. In fact, at the end of each of the first two months of their visits, she gave him forty cents for each non-cussing period. I could tell by the Frog's grins on those days that he was doggoned proud of his accomplishment.

Then, one late spring day, Froggie didn't come to school. And he didn't show up that afternoon at the Legion Field for our weekly big game with some of the high school guys. Granny stood at the window that afternoon—and for several afternoons beyond—watching for the sight of the disheveled boy walking head down, usually shivering in his ragged shirt and sweater, but nevertheless ambling purposefully toward our driveway. But he didn't come. He wasn't to come to our house again or to be seen in Post Oak ever again.

Granny inquired around and learned from Mr. Cope, the old peddler who lived out near the Roundbottom place, that Seth's shack was now deserted. According to Mr. Cope, the last time Seth was released from the county jail, he went home, loaded up a few miserable items in his piece-of-crap 1941 Ford sedan, told Froggie either "to git in or stay—don't matter to me none which-a-way" and then drove off. Froggie went with him. I reckon the devil you know is usually better than the devil you don't know. I reckon.

One not-so-reliable source declared that Seth and Frog had "lit out for Alabammy," perhaps in search of the wife and daughters who had left Post Oak several years before. Mr. Strawbridge vowed that Seth was so mad on the occasion of his most recent incarceration that he swore he'd "get the hell out of this shit-hole town and back to a place where I'm respected." Fat chance. But Landsford County was now purged of Roundbottoms.

My grandmother died in June of 1958, having contracted what was then termed "hardening of the arteries." Given the nature of this disease and its quick progression, it'd probably be diagnosed today as early onset Alzheimer's. Not long before the end, Granny would often drop pans and glasses in the kitchen, leave the water running in the bathroom lavatory, and pick up a small, ornamental, porcelain dish off the coffee table, place it to her ear, and carry on extended phone conversations with her best friend, Mrs. Annie Corley. Mrs. Corley had died two years before. Granny's funeral in Post Oak Methodist Church was held before a standing room congregation. Even the Baptists came.

Two years into my retirement, a business trip brought a good friend through Columbia, South Carolina, my home for the past forty years. He called me in the early afternoon and dropped by the house for a drink before resuming his drive to Charleston. This friend, Ron Morrell, and I had served together as training officers in an Army National Guard active duty assignment in Enid, Oklahoma, during the mid-1980s. Five or six years following our duty together, Ron found himself in an Army Reserve unit in Mississippi and was deployed during Operation Desert Storm. By the time of Ron's visit, both of us had retired from military service. We enjoyed catching up and laughing about the good work, good friends, and good times we'd experienced in Enid. As Ron was leaving, he stopped at the front door and seemed to struggle to recapture an important event or a name he wanted to share.

"Mike," he said after a short time, "did you ever know a guy from your home town in Post Oak named Jeremiah Roundbottom?"

I was startled and took a moment to gather myself and plug back in to the long ago time. "Why, yeah, I did," I said. "I think. Lord, I haven't thought about this fellow for a long, long time—if it's the same person. We always called him 'Froggie' and never knew his given name. I reckon *Jeremiah*'s appropriate, though. I'm remembering the early 70s song called *Jeremiah was a Bullfrog*. You remember it?"

"Yeah, I do," responded Ron. Then my friend stepped back into the foyer with me and appeared a bit sad. "Mike, were you and this guy good friends?"

"We were," I said, "but I actually think Froggie was closer to my grandmother than to me. It's a long story. How do you know Froggie?"

"Sergeant Roundbottom was one of our mess cooks in Iraq." Ron talked more slowly than he had during our reminiscing. "He was a hard worker and always seemed to appreciate his assignment and being in the Army. He was kind of a loner and a little strange. You know, that guy could use either hand to do anything—prepare country steak, dish out mashed potatoes, write up rations requests, shoot a basketball . . . anything." My friend became even more serious. "We had a few talks there in the mess tent after evening meals. When I learned he had lived in Post Oak, Georgia, I asked him if he had known you—just a long shot. He smiled and said he 'shore did' and asked if I knew how you were doin'. When I told him where you were and that you were a college English teacher, he chuckled and nodded his head and said he figured 'you'd make somethin' outta yoreself.' He seemed to like you a lot."

"Froggie was a sad case," I told Ron. "His folks didn't have the proverbial pot to pee in. His dad was a real butthole and treated him like crap. His mom and sisters had run off to South Alabama without him. My grandmother spent time with him, but one day he just disappeared, and we never heard from him again. Do you know how I can call him? Is he still in the Reserve in Mississippi?"

Ron decided not to mince words. "He's dead. You know, we didn't have too many casualties during that first Gulf War, but Roundbottom ran out of luck, I guess. One of Saddam's SCUDs fell into his mess tent, and all the guys inside—including Roundbottom—were killed." Ron waited for a minute for me to look down, sigh, and return to the conversation. "I'm sure this was your friend in Post Oak. Every now and then, I'd notice him with a green Sharpie drawing and writing on stuff. You know what he drew mostly?"

"Let me guess," I said. "Wide-mouthed frogs. He probably was drawing wide-mouthed frogs everywhere, wasn't he?"

Ron smiled a little and nodded. "Yep," he agreed. "He drew those damned frogs all over the place: on his magazines, inside his foot locker, on the margins of ration requests, and I had to chew his ass about that one. I even found one on the inside of his utility hat. I'm sorry to give you this news, Mike. Maybe I should have kept it to myself."

"Nope, I'm glad to know about Froggie." I continued, "I'm sure he was given a proper military funeral. Do you know for sure?"

"Yeah," said Ron. "We sent his body back to a little place near Dothan, Alabama. I think one of his sisters was responsible for the receipt of the remains. He was buried in the closest National Cemetery."

After Ron left, I went back into our den, mixed another drink, and sat down. My wife Charlotte came up behind me and placed her hands on my shoulders. "I heard the conversation at the door. I'm sorry about Froggie," she said. Her consolation was much appreciated.

"Thanks, Sweetie," I replied, reaching back to pat one of her hands. "You know, it sounds like the Frog pretty much made it out of that horrible situation he was born into. My dad used to say that all of us have to play the hands we're dealt, but sometimes, the damned deck seems to be stacked, doesn't it?" I took a last sip of bourbon and continued, "We really didn't think Froggie would ever be OK. It took a lot of fortitude for him to make it. I'm so very proud of him."

I rose slowly from my chair and ambled past Charlotte and into the kitchen. And, I thought, as I poured out the ice from my drink and switched off the remaining kitchen light, Granny would be proud, too.

The Trip to Chitlin' Creek

Mullet Kinlaw was being his usual know-it-all self that Sunday afternoon. We'd stopped passing the football and were sitting on the Kinlaw front steps. He'd already hinted that Peter Tom Robertson's sister had "done the big thing" with Cotton McAlister's truck driver cousin and that ol' man Cockwilder had been caught near Asheville, North Carolina, with a batch of bootleg fireworks and a bunch of packs of stolen cigarettes. I tried to change the subject, so I mentioned the possibility of a fishing trip. Mullet became excited. He responded, "Let's get our stuff and go on over to Chitlin' Creek. It ain't a-gonna rain today, I don't think. Tommy Birdsong told me at school that the bream are hittin' at Reeves Slough 'round that big ol' brush pile." Then Mullet sort of snickered. "We'll go, iffen you ain't afraid to climb down those big rocks at the slough."

This was typical Mullet. "I ain't afraid!" I replied, with rising anger. A kid's honor is indeed an important thing. Mullet remembered the day we'd gone to our fishing place and I'd slipped on a bed of mossy slime and slid right on into the creek. When you do something like that, you aren't allowed to forget it—ever. It's a rule. I calmed down a little and added, "You think Millard'll wanna go, too?" Millard was Mullet's older brother and was the starting center on the Post Oak High School football team. Following his senior season, he was good enough to be offered a full scholarship to play football at a small college in Alabama. But as if it were some sort of familial obligation, Millard treated his brother like doggie doo most of the time and seemed to resent having to share a bedroom with him. He considered Mullet and me to be pests, for the most part, and usually wanted nothing to do with us. But he knew stuff about bream fishing that we'd never know, and he was also good at finding worms in the pasture between our houses and the wooded pathway to the creek. We needed him a bunch more than he needed us. Maybe he'd go.

Mullet Kinlaw was a tall, lanky boy my age, nine, who didn't have many friends at school. He was born with one leg shorter than the other, so he walked around with a pronounced limp and tended to drag his long leg. You know how it is. Anything that makes you the least bit odd and different from everybody else in grammar school will make your socialization process a challenge. And so it was for Mullet. It didn't help that Mullet's defense mechanism was to be a smart aleck most of the time, even when the situation didn't call for it. He especially could be testy when some of our buddies branded him "Igor" and used this moniker over and over when the teacher wasn't paying attention. He rubbed most people the wrong way: his schoolmates, his teachers, the local Methodist and Baptist ministers, even, unfortunately, his own dad.

But it wasn't hard to rub Martin Kinlaw the wrong way. His wife could do it by just walking through the house. In fact, my grandmother and Mrs. Corley used to speculate that Mr. Kinlaw was physically abusive to all of his family before the time when such behavior was more investigated and less tolerated. The Kinlaw patriarch was the sales manager at the local Dodge place and was a huge sports fan. He was proud of Millard's football ability; without intent, I hope, he would compare Millard's talent to Mullet's shortcomings in ways that were hurtful. Yep, Millard was definitely the alpha brother. Mullet's smart-assiness was probably linked to his second-class citizen status at home as much as the constant teasing he received at school. With all that in place, my dad always used to say that a guy had to play the hand he was dealt.

We went through the front door of the Kinlaw house with reverence and care. On Sunday afternoon, Mr. Kinlaw would be stretched out on the sofa with a close-by Pabst Blue Ribbon and the TV already tuned in to the NFL game. In the 1950s in the television broadcasting area around Chattanooga, you didn't have the voluminous sports choices you have today with cable access, ESPN, ESPN2, the Golf Channel, and all those venues. You had channels for ABC, CBS, and NBC, and that's all. What you had on CBS on Sunday—and were glad of it—was the weekly Washington Redskins game. During this time, the Redskins were the NFL team closest to Chattanooga (My home town of Post Oak was a little over 18 miles south of Chattanooga just over the state line into Georgia.) and, therefore, this team's games were the ones sent to our viewing area. Plus, the Redskins were awful. They usually won two or three games a year over a twelve-game schedule. They went through several quarterbacks, but my favorite was "little Eddie LeBaron," who was not over 5' 6" tall and weighed right at 150 pounds. He would have been a decent passer if he could have seen over the large and mainly unblocked defensive ends who made his life miserable week in and week out. On this particular Sunday, we noticed the score on the scratchy black and white TV screen was New York Giants 28, Washington Redskins 3. The game was nearing the end of the first half. It could have been worse. Mr. Kinlaw growled something unkind as we walked by in his view, and then he repositioned himself on the sofa.

I reckon Mrs. Kinlaw was back in the kitchen preparing the next meal for her three hearty appetites. I don't remember seeing her. Anyway, we quietly went on through to the boys' room and grabbed the fishing stuff stacked in the corner.

Millard was hunched over the small desk near the window finishing some algebra homework. Without looking up, he threatened, "Whatta you assholes doin' with my rod and reel. Put that crap back."

"Come go fishin' with us, shitass," Mullet said. It's worth it to say that Mullet was always proud of any vulgar terminology he remembered to use, especially in front of his brother. As is obvious, the use of this colorful compound proved that brotherly love was rampant in the Kinlaw family. Anyway, my friend had learned this word from his brother only a couple of weeks back, and Mullet would throw it into conversations with abandon and without better discretion. He received ten licks the day he referred to our principal, Miss Horner, with this term but within her earshot. I tried to plead his case by stressing that this word *shitass* implied the masculine gender, but Miss Horner would have none of it. Mullet continued, "We're goin' down to the slough. Come on. We might get to see Lockhart slide into the creek again if we're lucky."

"Bite me," I responded to Mullet with no particular enthusiasm. "Bite me" was a sort of automatic come-back to your friends back then, at least for a while. Probably because we didn't quite grasp the intent of the phrase—or even where the biting would occur—we allowed this one to fall out of our daily vernacular.

"Aw, hell. I guess so," replied Millard. He was tired of algebra, and he also knew that no one would see him with his younger brother and a young buddy at the creek. To have one of Millard's peers see him doing anything with us other than frogging our arms or stuffing us into street corner garbage cans would brand Millard a wussy and would result in at least a week of constant ribbing. But he'd be safe with us at the creek. No one would see. He put on his dilapidated Converse All Stars tennis shoes, jerked his new fishing tackle out of Mullet's hands, and picked up his tackle box. "Don't ever use my stuff, you turd!" Millard hissed at his brother. "Now get us somethin' we can use for a worm can. Let's go."

Chitlin' Creek was one of those meandering, on again-off again creeks common to the rural South. This old, usually muddy tributary was shallow in most places but did provide us with swimming holes—complete with the obligatory rope swings—in a couple of isolated spots. And I recall several places along the creek where the wooded banks would show off their huge, leaning post oaks with exposed roots and scrub brush growing all around. Near town, Chitlin' Creek curved around the main local industry, Sweet Briar Rug Mill, and had become a convenient waste receptacle for Sweet Briar's unneeded carpet remnants, pieces of damaged looms, and left-over dyes. We thought it intriguing to visit the creek immediately following a dye dump. The chartreuse, deep burgundy, and light green colors transforming the muddy water were tints not to be found in nature. The resident carp, catfish, bass, bream, water moccasins, and snapping turtles were not enamored of this design change, either, and vacated the area quickly or went belly up. Somewhat later, when I was in college, my cousin, Mitch, won a science fair competition by completing a lot of environmental research, testing the waters of ol' Chitlin' Creek periodically over six months, and presenting his pollution project on several poster boards adorned with much narrative and fascinating color photos. A couple of guys from the Georgia Environmental Control Agency got wind of the project and talked with my cousin and his parents at the state competition in Atlanta. I understand that, when this word got around, Mitch's dad lost his spot on town council and became the butt of a number of crude comments about community loyalty. Nevertheless, our family felt strong pride in Mitch's intelligence, courage, early-on environmental awareness, and parental support.

It didn't take us too long to get to Reeves Slough. We'd stopped only once to dig some worms near the leaky water trough used by ol' man Trendle's cattle. The moisture around the trough and the cow piles made for a generous worm supply. We eventually worked our way to the creek bank by climbing slowly down, awkwardly holding our fishing stuff with one hand and grabbing onto roots and vines and dead tree trunks with the other. All in all, Reeves Slough was almost half a mile from our houses, and not many people knew about it. Much of the year, the slough was filled and drained down on a regular basis by the flow of Chitlin' Creek, but in the summer it was brackish and exuded a stagnant, decaying kind of smell that could stay with you if you happened to fall in. The day I slid into the slough ended in a full hour's bath with Granny scrubbing every part of me that could be scrubbed. It was downright embarrassing. At age nine, I was too old to have my grandmother taking part in my baths.

This day would turn out to be a good fishing day. The three of us must have caught 20 bream and two old one- to two-pound mud cats before we ran out of bait. I caught eight of the bream and both catfish myself, mainly, I think, because the Kinlaw boys were too busy cussing each other out to pay close attention to their bobbers. The best part by far, though, was Millard's turn to enter the slough.

Millard enjoyed lording his age, size, and coordination over Mullet and me, and he especially relished bragging noisily about this obvious multi-faceted superiority. He was belittling us as he pointed to a partly submerged pine tree and boasted that he'd put his hook and bobber directly under this tree. "There might be a big ol' bass just a-waitin' for my juicy worm right under that pine limb," Millard predicted. He casted aggressively, but his line wound around one of the topmost limbs. Not wanting to lose any of his tackle at all, he climbed out carefully and assumed an awkward perch on a protruding rock that adjoined the mostly underwater pine. He began to jerk his line hard, and with the third jerk, the line suddenly popped. Millard began to lose his balance and stumbled backward, yelling and cussing. He tottered back and forth on the slippery rock and reached desperately for Mullet. Now do you think Mullet was a big help? Mullet moved back a little so as to be just out of Millard's reach. As the beefy center piled into the dank water, Mullet could be seen rendering the single finger salute so much a part of our Southern upbringing. The water wasn't over Millard's head, but his weight carried him under for a few seconds. He came up spitting and spluttering and just sort of stood there, with brownish ooze seeping out of his shirt and running down his arms and through his hair. He was already beginning to stink.

"You know what this means, asshole," he said to Mullet in a remarkably calm voice. "I'm a-gonna beat the hog mess outta you big time. You coulda caught me up there. You're dead."

"Yeah, I know," Mullet said with a resigned reply. "But it'll be worth it. See, you ain't always as perfect as Dad thinks you are." He chuckled but, at the same time, extended a tree limb to Millard, and Mullet and I pulled the hefty boy back up on the bank. When Millard was back on reasonably solid ground, he turned to his brother and took two steps toward the cringing boy. Mullet had brought both arms over his face in the ultimate submissive posture. Somehow, unexplainably, Millard slapped Mullet's right arm but nothing more.

"Come on," the larger boy said. "Let's get our stuff and go on home. We been over here a long time, and the sun's beginnin' to set. They might already be a-callin' us." As we managed to climb back onto the pathway, I heard Millard say under his breath to Mullet, "Dad don't think I'm perfect. He's on my butt 'bout somethin' all the damn time. You know that. Don't say things like that."

"Yeah, OK," replied Mullet.

I might have mis-remembered this part of it, but it seemed to me that Mullet limped along a little closer to Millard as we walked briskly back toward home. My only child status would always prevent me from grasping these brother-to-brother dynamics. And I was blessed not to have an abusive father.

The half mile trip back wasn't particularly eventful. Probably the most memorable thing about it on this day was the rancid, dankish, sweaty odor emanating from Millard as we went along. I walked behind the two brothers and was a bit downwind, so to me Millard seemed to be getting even more ripe with each step. And there was more of a high school center to ripen up, you know. Then, after a good while, we arrived at the topmost point of Mr. Trendle's pasture, a point that overlooked my house and the Kinlaw house down below us. Our houses were about half a football field apart. Our vantage point was around 100 yards away from our houses, and we had a clear view of the whole area.

The three of us stopped cold at the same moment.

"Damn!" exclaimed Millard.

"Aw, hell!" was Mullet's reply.

"We're dead meat," I offered, not wanting to believe what I was seeing.

My house was the second one up the road toward the pasture past the Kinlaw place, a position that made it the first in our line of sight. It was one of a number of rental houses my folks moved to during my early years. Our two houses were the only two on this gravel road. The road connected to the main state highway that ambled through Post Oak and was only 200 feet inside Post Oak's town limits. On this auspicious day my driveway and yard were full of cars and people. While we watched, another car and the Landsford County Emergency Services pick-up came pretty fast up the driveway and pulled onto the grass near the carport. We could make out both sets of parents, my grandma, Sheriff Samuels and his chief deputy, two of my aunts, Police Chief Alston, three workers from the Barbeque Shack across the main highway, the head of the Post Oak volunteer fire department, and Dr. Cookman, the physician who had delivered most of us and was probably called in case this turned out to be a medical emergency. At least nine cars and the truck were now parked in our driveway, in the yard at odd angles, and even down the gravel road toward the Kinlaw house. We could hear a constant buzz—with frequent ups and downs—of concerned conversation punctuated by an occasional wail from Granny. I reckon her generation often felt the need to wail. Her yowls and other loud interruptions included our names—the three of us—almost at times as if recited in the past tense.

"Jesus," started Millard. "What the hell has caused all that? It's our fault, but what've we done?"

"Nothin' that I can think of," I said. "We just went fishin'."

Mullet started to tremble. He was indeed a brave smartass at school and with us, but he was scared to death of his dad. "I'm a-gonna really get it now," he sort of croaked. "This'll embarrass Dad. He's gonna strap me good. It hurts so much. I hate it! And I hate him!"

"Shut up!' his brother corrected. "You ain't suppose' to hate yore own father. God'll get you fer it."

"Wait a minute," continued Millard. "We seen Mom in the kitchen before we left the house." He grabbed Mullet's right arm. "Did you tell her we was a-goin' to the creek? Did you? Tell me quick!"

Mullet could only shake his head. Now he *was* crying hard.

"Lockhart, did you tell your folks we was a-goin' fishin'?" Millard was panicky and was beginning to lose his usual surly sense of cool.

"I must've fergot," I said. "I was in too big a hurry to get my stuff and meet y'all. My folks were all a-talkin' in the livin' room after dinner. Oh, God! I just fergot."

Millard was the oldest and knew he had to be in charge. The age factor puts you in charge in a situation like this. But I could tell Millard was searching for some way to deal with what we had done—or not done. He must have known that we'd all get busted for this, but his role of responsibility would put him on the most prominent hot seat. He breathed deeply then began, "Get down! Don't let'um see us. OK, guys. We got a choice. They ain't seen us yet. We can cut back into the woods, go back to the creek, and wait this thing out some more. After dark—or maybe by tomorrow mornin'—they'll be really worried and maybe even be more glad to see us when we walk down outta this here pasture. The women'll be cryin' and all, and Lockhart's grandma'll be a real mess. Maybe they'll ferget about bustin' us or findin' other stuff to do to us. Or . . . we can just stand up and walk down the pasture right now and take what's a-comin'. Whatta you think?"

Mullet was no help at all. He was blubbering all over himself and was by this time sitting down straddle-legged near a big rock. I finally responded, "I'll bet they'll come a-lookin' for us anyway with our dads and guys from the fire department and the sheriff's office. They'll go to the creek first. Hell, we can't get away from this. Besides it'll get kinda cold after dark, and we ain't got no jackets. And yore all wet and stinky, Millard. Let's just go on down and get it over with."

Millard was amazingly calm and agreeable. "Yeah, let's go," he said.

Mullet snuffled loudly, struggled to his feet with his brother's help, wiped his eyes and nose, and stood up as straight as he could. "OK," he said meekly. Sometimes the downfall of the resident smartass can become pitiful.

We were halfway down the pasture toward my house when Aunt Lucinda was the first to notice us. "Lord a-mercy," she almost screamed. "Lookee there. There come those precious lost sheep. There they are!"

Our parents, my grandma, and assorted other kin came running toward the ramshackle, loose-hanging gate that was our entry and exit point to Mr. Trendle's pasture. The gate was over across our front yard beyond a small brook that ran along the pasture fence. The other non-kin folks stayed in the yard to watch the fun. Mr. Kinlaw was the first to reach us as we maneuvered through the gate. Millard started to explain, but he didn't have much of a chance. The big boy's stench and wet condition coupled with the stringer of fish I carried gave away the afternoon's events. Mr. Kinlaw's huge hands grabbed each boy around the nape of each neck, and he pushed and drove and occasionally dragged my miserable buddies toward home. Mrs. Kinlaw followed, trying to pat each boy gently and softly letting them know how glad everyone was to see them. Each time she patted, her husband grumbled something profane and sort of kicked her away. Somehow, I was sure, her remonstrations would not offset the horror that was about to happen. And it got worse because, as I learned later, the Redskins had come back to beat the Giants 38-35 and Mr. Kinlaw had missed it because he had left his comfortable sofa and PBR to join the panicked delegation awaiting our return.

At pretty much the same time as the latching on of Mr. Kinlaw to his boys, my mother was the first to get to me. Granny was right with her. They both sort of hugged me and patted me and even kissed me and leaned heads against my skinny little shoulders. I was facing our house by this time, and Mom and my grandma were holding me and were facing back toward the pasture. For a couple of instants, I thought that maybe, just maybe, I'd come out of this one unscathed. Fat chance. As this hugging vignette unfolded, I can remember seeing my dad in front of me and only a few feet away. He reached out calmly and took my tackle box and rod and reel and stringer of fish. Then he smiled—in relief, I thought—but also in acknowledgement of what was to come. You see, unlike in the Kinlaw home, my dad was not the force of discipline at my house. It was Mom and Granny, in that order. The instrument of punishment was the proverbial hickory switch, fortunately never usually applied with maximum force. I had long since realized that a fake cry would mitigate the switch's application. The venue of punishment was our bathroom. It's a wonder I was ever properly potty trained.

Slowly, inexorably, Mom released from her tight hug and backed away. She looked at me with piercing eyes. Bill Cosby, prior to his fairly recent legal troubles, has a monologue in which he described his wife's anger at a moment of rage against their son and his surprising new Mohawk haircut. Cosby maintained that the skin around his wife's eyes and hairline tightened and appeared almost to begin to slide off her skull. Yep, that about describes it. Mom looked like that. She snarled, "Get inside and go straight to the bathroom. Now!"

By this time, my dad, still smiling, was no doubt glad that he didn't have the disciplinarian role. He had certainly been concerned about our whereabouts, but, at the same time, he probably had found the whole thing to be a bit humorous. Mom would counsel him on this attitude later. He thanked those who had gathered for the emergency and asked if anyone wanted a cup of coffee. Coffee was always brewing at our house. No one did. They all expressed their relief at our homecoming, returned to their cars, and convoyed back down the gravel drive to the main highway. As the last car, Dr. Cookman's, moved out of sight, the noise of tires on gravel subsided. I walked ahead of Mom, slowly opened the back door, stopped for a minute, and thought I heard the sounds of a belt strap and desperate, timed screams coming from the Kinlaw place. As bad as it was going to be, I preferred Mom and the hickory switch. I might even pretend to cry more loudly this time.

The Lizard in the Library

One early North Georgia spring day in the trees near Chitlin' Creek, I happened across a fence lizard groggy from his recent hibernation. They do hibernate, you know. He was lethargic and sort of bunched up with his legs tightly underneath his thin body. He had climbed about four feet up the side of an old oak tree, and his scraggly, brown-flecked and grayish skin was good camouflage for a skinny little fellow barely ten inches long, tail and all. He tried to bite me only once when I picked him up. I was between pets at the time and felt that I needed an animal of some sort to be my pal and hang around with me after school. This reptile was my ticket to a new four-legged friend as well as an item of interest for my classmates at Post Oak Grammar School. I invited the lizard into my two-tray tackle box, closed and latched the lid, picked up my Zebco rod and baitcasting reel combo, and started off toward home.

A couple of things needed to be decided right away. First, the lizard had to have a name. One of my friends was Ralph Moreland, a guy who was at least five years older than me and yet still deigned to hang out with me (or to let me hang out with him). Moreland would even double me on his bicycle around our fair town many afternoons. At other times, we would build plastic model cars together in the attic work shop at his house. Come to think of it, Moreland must not have had many friends near his age. Anyway, I thought I'd name the lizard "Ralph" both as a way to thank my buddy and as a kind of reminder of Moreland's glazy reptilian eyes. Secondly, Ralph must have a home. It didn't take long for me to find a shoe box, punch a few air holes in the lid, collect and spread some leaves and grass and sticks and a small rock or two, and fashion a water bowl out of the top off a jar of peanut butter. A few days later, my mom wasn't overly impressed to find a topless jar of dried out peanut butter in the pantry, but she accepted this phenomenon with a resigned sigh as she usually did when I screwed up. I also squished a couple of flies and one small black beetle and scattered the remains around the bottom of the shoe box. Ralph was then deposited into the box and seemed generally OK with his situation. I checked on him several times a day and at least once at night. Amazingly enough, because he came not to hide quickly each time I opened the box lid, I assumed he was getting used to me. He probably was growing weak from malnutrition and dehydration since fence lizards don't thrive in shoebox captivity, but I didn't know. After all, while he didn't flourish, he did survive.

But the pet experience of a fence lizard in the shoebox rapidly became not too exciting. During recess one day, it came to me. In the spirit of a nine-year-old's revelation, I envisioned Ralph as being able to accompany me around Post Oak! Yeah! This would be wonderful! My buddies would get to see Ralph every day, and those mouthy and pesky girls would be scared to death! What fun! One problem: how would I secure Ralph while at the same time presenting him for full view? I figured this out, too. I could gently tie a piece of string around Ralph's small belly, tie the other end to a paper clip, and wear Ralph attached to my lapel by means of the fastener part of the paper clip. He would be on a sort of special reptile leash. In this way, I could easily make Ralph my companion and be able to remove him—firmly secured, of course—for treks around my room at home, on my desk at school, and around other places such as my mom's office and the dime store toy counters. I'll tell you, no one else at Post Oak Grammar School owned a leashed pet lizard. Goodness! I hope no SPCA types are even now thinking of some sort of eternal punishment for me.

After school on a Tuesday almost three months into my association with Ralph, Will Weaver, my best friend, and I decided to walk over to McEachern's drug store for a couple of packs of baseball cards. We knew that Dr. McEachern was the first in Post Oak to order new batches of cards, and we had figured out also that Topps Chewing Gum Company printed cards by series instead of by some sort of random selection. This meant that you might be able to buy only the first 150 or so cards in the set from stores that wouldn't re-order until the previous supply was gone. This year, 1956, the Topps set contained 340 cards. You'd get the same Wally Westlakes, Nelson Burbrinks, and Danny O'Connells over and over because the store owner didn't have enough card business to deplete the early series issues and he wouldn't buy more. It was a vicious cycle: the stores get in the early series cards; we buy them until we'd collected almost all of these early issue players; we stop buying; the store owner won't re-order because he still has several unopened boxes of these early cards left; no one in Post Oak is able to complete sets because we're never able to purchase the last couple of series, probably 100-150 more non-duplicate cards; we're all pissed. And, to top it off, many of the best players of the time—Mickey Mantle, Willie Mays, Gil Hodges, Roy Campanella, Whitey Ford, Eddie Mathews—were invariably included in these later series.

I suspect that my dilemma has to do with living in a small town. The larger cities had larger markets of kids buying cards, so the stores ran through more boxes, re-ordered more often, and made entire sets available to their eager customers. Don't shrug and take out your cellphone. This is important stuff. You don't learn about baseball card distribution problems in the 1950's by watching *Captain Kangaroo, Have Gun Will Travel, Lawrence Welk, Leave It To Beaver,* or *The Donna Reed Show.* It's amazing the kinds of things that matter to kids who are seven, eight, nine years old and have few diversions in their complicated but often boring lives. Weaver and I did know, I must emphasize, that if newer cards were to be had, Dr. McEachern's drug store was the likeliest place in Post Oak to have them. Don't ask me why. Maybe Dr. McEachern had figured out the Topps distribution formula and felt sorry for us.

On our way down Cleburne Street, we were stopped by two younger kids who wanted to see Ralph. I let them on the condition that there would be no touching. Ralph disliked touching, even mine. Willing enough to comply, these kids went away amazed that someone they knew (1) would stop to show them a lizard and (2) would be brave enough to let the lizard crawl around on his neck and go under his shirt. After this encounter, I noticed Weaver in deep thought, quite an accomplishment for him. "People like Ralph and are interested in 'em, ain't they?" Weaver finally observed.

"Yep, I reckon so," I replied. "I'm thinkin' 'bout turnin' him loose, though. He'd probably be a lot happier back in the woods, and, besides, I don't think he's been eatin' many of the dead bugs I'm givin' him. Dad told me lizards are better off out in nature—that's where they're suppose' to be. You wanna go with me over to Chitlin' Creek later?"

"Yeah, I guess so." Weaver was sort of sad, I thought, that we needed to say good-bye to our little friend. We were both quiet for a while as we walked on to the drug store. Then he stopped abruptly. "But let's have a little fun with Ralph before he goes!" Weaver blurted out.

"Whadda you mean?" I asked, kind of suspicious that Weaver might have something bad in mind for our reptile pal. "I ain't a-doin' nothin' that will hurt Ralph," I declared, beyond, I figured, keeping him tied pretty tightly to a string, making him live in a shoebox, and feeding him dead bugs.

"Hell no, Lockhart, we ain't a-gonna hurt him. I wouldn't do that," responded Weaver. "So far, we've protected ol' Ralph and shown him off just to our buddies, ain't that right?"

"Yeah, and our parents. I tried to show him to Aunt Rebecca yesterdy, but she ran out of the room and yelled for mama. Older women don't like lizards at all. I got in trouble for that. I ain't a-gonna do nothin' like that again," I stated with firmness.

"Let's take Ralph to the li-berry and show 'em to Aunt Maud. This'll be great! She'll yell and jump around and stuff, like your Aunt Rebecca, and a lot of kids will be in the li-berry to see it. Hot damn! This'll be great!" Weaver was beside himself that he'd thought of this idea and now couldn't wait to put it into practice.

It's worth saying at this point that Weaver's aunt, Miss Maud Dickson, was the county librarian and had been since 1930 or so. She was a prim and proper, strong postured, late middle-aged, unmarried, educated lady who prided herself on self control, vast knowledge of books for kids and even adults, and strict discipline in her library at all times. She ran a correct and well-organized shop. No one could misbehave, talk too loudly, or mishandle books at all. In fact, she even spent a lot of time thumbing through all returned books to make sure no damage was apparent. She'd return any downturned page corners to their rightful places and try to press out the crease. Now who'd take time to do that? Really, as far as we knew, no one had ever tried to mess with Miss Dickson or talk back to her in any way, shape, form, or fashion. Her one weakness, if you want to call it that, was an uncontrollable fear of crawly things or things that could fly and could come out and surprise you and even get on you, things like wasps, roaches, mice, silverfish, toads, snakes of any size, and, we were about to find out, lizards. To smart talk her or interfere with her precise world would be to incur her wrath and a follow-up phone call to your mom. In Post Oak, Georgia, in 1956, if you screwed up with a (the) librarian, teacher, shopkeeper, cook at the Chow Place, or just about anyone in authority, you got your little ass chewed by the adult immediately affected by your screw-up then you'd get busted at home because the affected adult would call your house long before you could get there to explain it. I reckon this system existed in most small Southern towns in the 1950s.

"So, OK, how 'bout it? Let's go to the li-berry!" Weaver was excited big time. "Shit's bells!" (When you're just on the cusp of learning to cuss, you often mix metaphors.), he exclaimed. "This 'un go down in history! No one's ever messed with Miss Maud in the li-berry! They'll be talkin' about this 'un when we're in high school!"

I was a bit less enthusiastic. "Do ya know what kinda trouble we'll get in?" I asked seriously. "Your dad'll rip you a new 'un. My grandmother'll jerk me into the bathroom at the house, and I hate goin' into the bathroom with her. She keeps a hickory switch on top of the refrigerator for really bad stuff, and this 'un will be really bad. My butt'll get striped, and I won't get to mess around after school for weeks."

Weaver wasn't convinced. He and I had long ago moved to that stage of kid-ness where we were smart enough to evaluate things. You know what I mean. You know you'll get switched and even more for doing something you aren't supposed to do, but the act is possibly enough fun to be worth the switching. Playing tackle football after school in your good school clothes is an example. You're supposed to go to your room and change clothes and you'll probably get whipped if you don't, but the clothes change is time wasted. So you risk a torn pocket or ripped off buttons or permanent mud stains. Ralph in the county library? Hmmm . . . maybe this would fall into the "worth it" category. "I don't know, Weaver. This could get us into big trouble. And, hey, Miss Dickson's your own kin. You don't mind messin' with your own aunt?"

"Ah, hell, Lockhart. You're a chicken. We can't pass this up. I'll bet Ralph would like it, too. Besides, ever time Aunt Maud comes to our house for dinner or somethin', she says somethin' to make me look bad 'cause I don't read much. Then Mama crawls my butt when Aunt Maud goes home. Naw, I don't mind messin' with her a-tall." Weaver wanted this one in a big way.

"I think we'd better just get the ball cards and go on home," I almost begged.

"Lockhart, you chicken, I double-dog dare you to take Ralph to the li-berry and put him on Aunt Maud's big ol' desk. You ain't got a hair on your ass if you back out." Neither of us had acquired ass hair yet. I suspect Weaver had heard his big brother Josie say this at some point, and Josie was seventeen, so you wanted to repeat stuff he'd say. And Weaver's statement was more compelling than usual: a double-dog dare put you in a bad situation. If you didn't accept it, you definitely *were* a chicken. Weaver, while my best friend, was also the type of person who'd talk about my cowardice at school the next day and at little league practice. Crap! What's a guy to do?

"OK. OK," I caved. "This'll probably make us famous any-way. We ain't had much fun around here lately—maybe since ol' man Cockwilder was arrested for bootleggin' firecrackers and cherry bombs over behind the fire station. But we stay together on this 'un, right?"

"Sure. Sure," Weaver confirmed, already leading the way to the court house with the old county library in its basement. "I'll go in first and get Aunt Maud payin' 'tention to me while you get Ralph off your shirt and onto her desk. She needs to be surprised when she sees our lizard." Weaver, it seems, had long since taken a proprietary interest in Ralph.

The court house was a prominent building in Post Oak, maybe the most prominent. Guarded proudly by the north-facing Confederate soldier on the monument on its front lawn, the court house needed repairs—or even replacement—by 1956, but it'd been built the year the Civil War started, and our town leaders were too proud of it to consider seriously a major change. The old red brick building had been spared by the yankee general Sherman when this antichrist-type figure (to most Georgians) began his Atlanta Campaign in 1864. He didn't torch the court house because, as the story goes, the local Masonic lodge met on the second floor. Sherman, as a dedicated Mason, would not allow damage to this shrine of a meeting place. In town, he also selfishly and wisely saved the stately old antebellum Norris house to use as his winter headquarters, the First Baptist Church to use as a field hospital, and the railroad depot to use for offloading troops, supplies, and ammunition. They say that the rest of Post Oak was resplendent in a reddish-yellow glow as it burned for hours after Sherman's rear guard marched south in April of 1864.

The county library took up a good-sized portion of one part of the court house basement. When you entered the door at the end of the hall downstairs, you'd notice first the dank, damp, musty smell of old books, months behind magazines, and well-used newspapers, the *Atlanta Journal* probably the pick of the litter. Miss Maud Dickson's desk sat ahead of you and a little off to the left. She always sat in an enormous swivel chair as she reigned supreme over her domain. Fully stocked bookcases were placed behind her, limiting her range of motion and preventing her from moving backwards at all. She should be praised for using every available inch to its maximum advantage in her small library world. Adjoining Miss Maud's desk on the far side was a two-unit, dark oak, card catalog. It was about three feet taller than the desk and was over six feet long and almost three feet wide. Many labeled trays took up the space in this old relic. You see, most folks don't know about card catalogs nowadays, but these imposing cabinets were the heart and soul of all libraries—from school to county to large city to university—back before sophisticated software enabled a much more convenient circulation check-out and inventory tracking system. Miss Maud was proud of this old system—she knew nothing else—and delighted in helping her clients locate books and the other quite limited media resources through the enigmatic Dewey Decimal code on each catalog card. A few drawers in the catalog even provided space for the dated check-out slips from the back pocket of each book.

Moving around the library, we'd see new arrival books, such as they were, resting in a small stand about six feet in front of Miss Maud's desk. As I recall today, the library was one big room, subdivided by bookcases and a couple of large reading tables. The place always seemed dark to me, too dark for clear reading to go on for long. The book shelves closed in on all sides of this area, and one prone to claustrophobia might do well to send a proxy to check out materials.

One other item of interest was important to many of us. Along a far wall beneath the library's only small window was an old wooden easel holding a thick piece of matt board covered with heavy blue construction paper. This focal point marked the progress of all of us kids who participated in the summer reading club. Probably thirty-forty of us were involved. The title at the top of this clever display read "Landsford County's Trip to the Moon." Each kid was given a small cardboard spaceship with his or her name on it. Enough room was left below the name for the kid to pin a number representing the books read by that point in the summer contest. As you read books and reported the number to Miss Dickson, the proud librarian would pat you gently on the head, move over to the moon trip board, update your book tally, and reposition your spaceship through the stars and sky at an upwards place closer to the moon. The moon, you see, was immediately under the title at the top of the board. This was our revered goal: to reach the moon. And with this lunar victory came a coveted $10.00 gift certificate to McEachern's drug store. At the time of Ralph's visit—yep, you guessed it—my spaceship was ahead of them all! But as the Apollo 13 astronauts were destined not to walk on the moon's surface well over a decade later, neither was my scrawny little butt providentially to be the first to reach Landsford County's moon. Alas!

The Weaver-Lockhart plan worked to perfection that early summer day, perhaps causing more of a fabulous end product than even our wildest dreams could have predicted. Weaver executed his part effectively: he walked directly to his aunt and engaged her in the best Eddie Haskell-type conversation I'd ever heard. "Aunt Maud, thanks for givin' me a ride home yesterdy. It was rainin' hard, and I'd a-gotten my new shoes all muddy. Mama 'preciated it a bunch. Have you had a good day?"

"I have, I really have, Will," she responded. "I've had a lot of customers." With her eyes glued somewhat politely, somewhat suspiciously on her favorite nephew, she continued, "How's your mother's bursitis coming along? Is she getting over it by now? Bless her heart, she's been coping with that problem for a long time. I suppose it runs in our family." Miss Maud cast a couple of furtive glances my way as she talked with Weaver. She probably wondered why I was so cautiously approaching her desk while remaining kind of aloof. She moved forward a bit in her chair, folded her hands in front of her, and continued to stare at me. She had much room to spread her hands out on her desk because her anal retentive tendency toward neatness made it impossible for anything actually to be on the desk. This situation added to the specialness of Ralph's impending visit.

Then, struggling a bit to divert Miss Dickson's focus, Weaver pointed to the reader's club board across the room and asked, "Aunt Maud, is Michael still ahead over there? Do ya think anybody can catch'm? He loves to read. I wish I did. My spaceship's still on the launchin' pad." She followed his attention toward the spaceship board and away from me. He laughed with a fake gusto and continued to keep his aunt's focus on the board. My chance had arrived.

I had already removed Ralph's paper clip from my lapel and was gingerly holding the little guy in my left hand while my right hand held on to the clip leash. Ralph seemed surprised to be disattached from his normal vantage point and moved his creviced little head from side to side. Then I gently put him down on Miss Maud's desk, sort of toward where she was sitting as she conversed with Weaver and with her head turned away from me. Her desk was always so neat and orderly, I thought, as I leaned over to give Ralph more room to walk. Ralph was usually given about a foot of play on his leash so he wouldn't feel so trapped, and by this point he was at full tether. The clean, unencumbered, tidy desk was a grand stage for Ralph's personal guest appearance, and, to his credit, the little fellow took full advantage. He began to waddle across closer to Miss Dickson, and I let him do it. As was a popular saying around twenty years following this 1956 event, "The defecation was about to hit the circular wind machine."

When Miss Maud turned back to face me at the opposite end of her desk from Weaver, two things happened almost simultaneously. She at first politely nodded to me and began, "Oh, Michael, I hope you're . . . ." She got this far when the second thing occurred. She saw Ralph. To his credit, he looked directly at this imposing woman, opening his mouth and not appearing at all afraid. He even took two more side-to-side wiggles in her direction. In the same motion, Miss Maud awkwardly moved sideways and up out of her chair. The swivel chair allowed this dual maneuver, even if it did complain with a loud squeak. It was the noise from Miss Maud that was really special. What came from her at first sounded like a grunting hiss from a zombie in a class "B" movie. It's funny how you notice the small things at a time like this. I noticed, as Miss Maud twisted in her chair, a dab of spittle beginning to form at the right side of her mouth. It was no doubt unintended and not Southern lady-like.

The next part of the Ralph visit was far beyond anything we thought would happen. You have to know, however, that Weaver, the five other kids, and the two adults in the library at the time will confirm this next event—and did confirm it all over Post Oak for the next two months to anybody who'd listen. Miss Maud's vocalizing had by this point become a shrill, whistling, sporadic scream. Then, I swear to God, Miss Maud jumped onto her desk and quickly placed one leg over the top of the card catalog in, as they say, one fell swoop. This scrambling movement would have been classy for Pee Wee Reese but was quite adroit for a woman pushing sixty. She pulled her other leg to the top of the cabinet and watched Ralph with horror. By this point, she loomed over us like a large, crouching, predatory bird. She finally managed to say, "What . . . what is that thing? What's it doing in my library?" She was breathing really hard by this time. And I had not had the good sense to remove Ralph. I just looked at Miss Maud with absolute amazement and found myself admiring her athleticism.

Weaver found his voice first. "That's Ralph, Aunt Maud. He's Michael's pet lizard. He ain't a-gonna hurt you. Ain't he great? Do you wanna hold him?"

This wasn't a wise question to ask a proper Southern lady who had just a moment before exhibited her fright and well-coordinated if unladylike climbing skill. Two of those present that day would later swear that Miss Maud peed on herself, but this part remains unproven and generally unspoken. Miss Maud was making a low gurgling sound and eventually uttered in a raspy whisper to the two adults, "For God's sake, help me off here. If I fall, I'll break a leg."

I now quickly retrieved Ralph and returned him to my lapel. Weaver and I didn't know what to say or do. We'd expected a bit of fright, maybe a mild scream and then a laugh, perhaps an awkward escape from her closed-in desk situation. But nothing like this. As Miss Maud worked her way down from the card catalog, I said, "Miss Dickson, I suppose you don't care to hear that I've finished readin' *All About Dinosaurs*, a biography of *Robert E. Lee*, and *Little Men*. Maybe I'll move up a couple of stars on the moon board?"

No, she didn't care. She pointed to the library's door and weakly muttered, "Both of you leave this library this instant. Don't come back for the rest of the summer. And both of your spaceships will be removed from the reading club contest. And I shall call your mothers this minute."

I'll bet you can guess how the rest of this day went. We went over to McEachern's and bought a few nickel packs of ball cards. A little later, trying to avoid the inevitable return to our houses, Weaver and I traipsed on over to Chitlin' Creek, found a large enough pine tree, untied Ralph from his leash, and placed the little guy near a small limb about five feet up. He stood still for a minute, peered back at us with disbelief, and sidled around the limb and up the tree until we couldn't see him anymore. I guess fence lizards don't develop strong emotional attachments to worthless, nine-year-old, junior buttholes. We watched for a couple of minutes. Then Weaver said, "Man! Did you see the ol' woman move? She was on top of the catalog cabinet so quick that she caused a run in her hosieries. Whatta sight!" He paused for a good while. "I reckon I won't be goin' to any famly gatherins' any time soon," he said with a sadness not becoming of Weaver.

I reflected with little attention to my friend, "I wonder if my grandmother or mama will switch me this time? I threw that last ol' hickory out into the back yard, but Granny'll get another one from the ol' shrubs on the side of the house. It'll be really sticky and hard and sharp 'cause those bushes are beginnin' to die. Damn! I reckon it's worth it. But, you know, ever time we come to the end of somethin' like this, I sorta regret that we did it. Sorta. . . . regret . . . Nah, it's worth it. Let's go home."

Froggie and the Stuck Truck

R oute 66 through the midwest and west gets all the nostalgic attention, the adventure programs on television, the promotion of fast muscle cars, and the once popular songs, but we have highways in the South that are every bit as important. For example, Highway 41 is a once heavily traveled north-south artery that plies its way through Post Oak, my home town in northwest Georgia. It snakes from somewhere in Michigan all the way to Miami, Florida, and, for well over forty years, it was a prime route for vacationers headed for the Sunshine State, for businessmen scheduling meetings in Atlanta, and for the giant eighteen-wheelers that were—and are—the backbone of our interstate commerce system.

Ol' "41 highway," as the Post Oakians call it, is still there; it just doesn't handle the volume of traffic it once handled, and it doesn't cater to its users the way it once did. Abandoned motels, bedraggled trailer parks, deserted roadside zoos formerly featuring abused black bears and sub-quality chenille bedspreads, souvenir stands selling cheap plastic Cherokee tomahawks and canoes made in Japan, and crumbling gas stations now litter this previously well-traveled and well-tended thoroughfare. The presence of so many of these unsightly structures—as well as their accompanying rotting billboard signage—is sad testimony to this route's previous status.

The advent of I-75, now three lanes each way between Chattanooga and Atlanta, quickly replaced 41 highway as a significant national interstate. But ol' 41 retains its share of good stories about ghostly hitchhikers, gutsy drag races orchestrated by drunk high school boys in '49 and '50 Mercs and '57 Chevys, horrific wrecks on dead man's curve near the 41 Truck Stop, and the milder and even slightly humorous events that have always been part of the culture of greater Post Oak.

In the mid-1950s, 41 highway shot almost gun barrel straight from the northern city limits of Post Oak near Longman's Lumber Company to the southern city limit sign just beyond Raeford's Gulf Station about a mile from town on the other end. It was enclosed for almost three-quarters of a mile by Post Oak proper, and it's not at all odd that our main business section, churches, gas stations, doctors' offices, the Bank of Post Oak, and even the court house were built on either side of this highway. The part of 41 highway that ran through Post Oak was named Cleburne Street not long after the Civil War to honor a Confederate general whose rear-guard delaying action at Post Oak Crossroads stalled Sherman's massive army for several days and probably enabled most of Joe Johnston's Army of Tennessee to retreat safely to Kennesaw Mountain near Atlanta. As I recall, only one obstacle kept all of the high-volume traffic from always moving efficiently through Post Oak: an underpass near our 1843-era train depot.

Forty-one highway moved directly under this rather narrow and not tall enough rock passageway. As the large tractor-trailer trucks grew even larger toward the end of the 1940s and as the load capacity of these behemoths expanded, it followed logically that the length and height of the trailers would also expand. Accommodating with ease the far fewer and smaller tractor-trailers that came through town during the 1930s, the underpass became unsuitable into the late 1940s and 1950s.

Unfortunately, the money was simply not available to realign the train tracks and raise the clearance of the underpass. The Post Oak town fathers solved the problem in the best way they knew how: they established and marked a detour that handled truck traffic coming from the north or south. Tractor-trailers traveling south were routed through a series of right angle turns, eventually re-accessing 41 highway approximately 800 feet to the north of the underpass near Raeford's Gulf Station. North-bound trucks would reverse this process. My family experienced this detour plan nightly because we lived for a time right on the detour route. The constant, late night grunting sound of downshifting and the swoosh of air brakes of Kenilworth, Peterbilt, and Mack rigs were annoying, but I reckon we got used to it.

Of course, this detour was marked clearly for trucks traveling north or south, with large signs posted at the city limits on both ends of town alerting the truck drivers to a lower in-town speed as well as to the need to follow a detour. I never felt the north end detour sign was as effective, though, because it was placed in the middle of one of those sequential Burma-Shave Brushless Shaving Cream advertising trails. This rhymed, clever signage read, "Henry the Eighth . . . Sure Had . . . Trouble . . . TRUCK DETOUR AHEAD . . . Short Term Wives . . . Long Term Stubble . . . BURMA SHAVE!" Or something like that. If a truck driver were lulled into the passing boredom of Burma Shave, he might miss the alert. And that inattention was what caused the mess on one otherwise bland day.

This mess by no means needs elaborate description. Briefly, early one Tuesday afternoon, a road weary truck driver failed to heed the TRUCK DETOUR AHEAD sign north of town, drove obliviously through Post Oak, and slowly entered the underpass. His tractor made it; his trailer didn't. Those working at the Pure Service Station and Owens Feed and Seed near the underpass swear that the screeching made by the trailer's top as it ground to a stop was akin to the amplified sound of a hundred fifth-grade boys scraping their unkempt finger nails across Mrs. Harper's blackboard at the Post Oak Grammar School. It was awful! Pieces of concrete fell on top of the trailer and to the pavement beneath. The tin of the trailer's top peeled back in four places. The driver abruptly stopped and got out to survey the damage. Already, the traffic was beginning to congest.

As is always the case when a small town is gifted with an out-of-the-ordinary event, much activity began simultaneously. All of the folks working closely enough to see or hear the stuck truck "came a-runnin'," as Granny used to say. Chief Alston pulled Post Oak's one police car, siren blasting, to a point behind the trailer and kept the red light atop the black and white 1956 Plymouth blinking brightly to signal oncoming traffic to stop. Several customers from the Dixie Diner dropped their forks and left Aunt Lattie's meatloaf specials to rush down the street toward the excitement. The clientele in Markson's Barber Shop—including the barbers, Joe and Wellman Markson—left their posts, too, for a look see. Cousin Thornton drove down to see what had happened then returned quickly to his ESSO station. He locked up the station's front door, jumped into the only tow truck in town—his beat up 1948 Ford F-Series pickup with a modified block and tackle towing contraption welded into the bed—and sped to the scene. The audience members for this rapidly assembling drama were about to get their money's worth.

The town fathers are to be commended for thinking up the truck detour idea, even if they were helped by the Georgia Department of Transportation. For the most part, it worked. But Mayor Reynolds and the town council stopped short of developing a work-around in case the detour plan slightly fizzled one day. And it fizzled mightily on the day this large

Kenilworth tractor and Swift Quality Meats refrigerated trailer came to an immediate, grating, scratchy-sounding halt half way through the underpass. By the time Will Weaver and I had bicycled over to the scene, everything had really cranked up. I was doubling Froggie Roundbottom on my bike, by the way. Ol' Seth Roundbottom couldn't afford to buy enough food for Froggie and him, much less a used bicycle for his son. Even so, we accepted the Frog as one of us and didn't mind doubling him around town on our bikes.

A crowd of nearly fifty Post Oakians had gathered with intense and noisy interest. The truck driver was being yelled at by Chief Alston, Mayor Reynolds, Commissioner Quinn, a Georgia Highway Patrolman who happened along and had stopped his car—with red light also flashing—next to Chief Alston's Plymouth, and several near-by travelers who were not so patiently waiting for someone to un-stick the truck. By this time the back-up of cars was growing large—in both directions. One guy from Ohio was practically screaming out his car window that if he didn't get to his Atlanta meeting on time, there'd be hell to pay! A nicer family from Kentucky had emerged from a wood-trimmed Ford station wagon to check out the hold-up. Other drivers started blowing their horns. This was great! I guess no one had figured out that a cooperative backing up and turning effort would have enabled these jammed up folks to follow the truck detour to a clear highway. Weaver and I decided not to mention it, and Froggie seemed perplexed by the whole situation and was "a-layin' low in de briar patch," as Br'er Rabbit does to avoid Br'er Fox in the wonderful Uncle Remus story. Besides, it's more entertaining to watch the adults lose it when something unexpected happens.

Thornton pulled up about that time in his red tow truck with "Turnbuckle's ESSO" painted in flaking gold lettering on both doors. He had driven around the detour to come out on the south side of the underpass and in front of the Kenilworth tractor. My dad always thought our cousin, Thornton, was a bit "too proud of what he knew" and wasn't reluctant to share his knowledge in a pompous way with those around him, and the rest of the family and numerous townspeople shared Dad's view. Anyway, it was even more fun to watch as Uncle Thornton hitched up his well-used tow bar and chain to the Kenilworth's front bumper, gave the chain a macho yank to test its tightness, and re-entered his tow truck. A couple of the closest backed-up motorists slightly applauded to watch someone—at least someone—try to help the situation. Now it takes little judgment to know that an old Ford pickup doesn't have enough oomph in its high mileage, 1948, flat-head V-8 to pry loose a huge tractor-trailer crammed against a concrete underpass. Anyone seeing the old red Ford would know that. The pickup's rear wheels only spun helplessly as Thornton gave it the gas.

He stayed with it, sadly, a little too long, and the rusty tow chain broke in two places. This quick and unexpected release of the fully taut chain plunged the pickup straight forward and into the first waiting car on the south side of the underpass. No one was hurt, but the driver, a well-heeled lady from Savannah and impatient to return home, was exceedingly pissed. She assured Thornton that her lawyer would be in touch with him and the mayor before the day ended—but she provided this assurance in advance of her discovery that Thornton owned the only repair shop in town able to fix the 1955 Cadillac the Savannah woman was driving. She soon calmed down a bit but wasn't about to let Thornton off the hook. Good! He needed to dangle for a while.

There's a frenetic crowd scene in *Gone with the Wind* in which Atlanta citizens are running to and fro amidst the crashing, galloping caissons and cannon and quartermaster wagons of John Bell Hood's repositioning Confederate army. Dogs and horses and even cattle belonging to refugees are intermingled with these loaded wagons, wounded soldiers in gray and butternut, and even a horse-drawn fire brigade. Scarlet runs through all of this trying to get back to Aunt Pitty-Pat's house. It's all chaotic and distressful. Vaguely similar, the Post Oak crowd scene on the day of the stuck truck wasn't dangerously out of control, but the din of shouting first responders coupled with the rising curses and horns from the rapidly expanding bottleneck of 41 highway traffic competed nicely with Hood's confused retreat. The drivers of oncoming cars were even trying to find other routes—both ways—around the back-up, and these folks were entangling the side streets of our fair hamlet. Many other drivers by this time were hanging loosely from their car doors, cursing creatively, and threatening all manner of horror toward the town fathers and town treasury. Weaver and I were amazed by this boisterous display of adult behavior and knew we'd have a lot to talk about at school. And then it was that Froggie, deciding to leave his self-imposed, secure briar patch, stepped toward the truck driver, Mayor Reynolds, and Chief Alston.

By the time of the stuck truck incident, Froggie Roundbottom had become a well-known figure to most in Post Oak. He and his dad were batching it in a beat up shack near Rising Buck, Mrs. Roundbottom having taken the girls and left for Alabama some five years earlier. She'd had it. Seth was a worthless redneck who never seemed to hold a job, relied on his popular recipe for moonshine to get them by, and would often violently take out his frustrations on Froggie. As the truck was maintaining its wedged-in status, ol' Seth was a guest of the county for thirty days owing to yet another unsuccessful "blue light special" with the discount price of his moonshine. Mrs. Strawbridge, the wife of the county's jailor, once again was giving the Frog room and board in the jail's storage closet while Seth finished his sentence.

Froggie was a good two years older than the rest of us, having failed first grade twice. But despite his lackluster academics and the shambles of his living conditions, he was one of the best baseball players at Post Oak Grammar School. Prior to after-school pick-up games, Frog was always the first one selected following the "throw the bat" method of choosing up sides. He was ambidextrous in both hitting and throwing, a talent no one in Post Oak had ever seen. He also was our advisor and consultant on many important matters: smoking rabbit tobacco; learning to cuss with verve and aplomb; providing needed tidbits about the facts of life, even if some of this stuff was flat wrong and anatomically impossible; and knowing when Mr. Cockwilder would bring in bootleg fireworks from North Carolina. He possessed as well a solid, common sense way of looking at things and fixing things and solving problems. He was fast at reattaching bicycle chains and replacing window panes broken due to errant throws or swings of the bat. If we supplied the needle and thread, he could even sew buttons back on or repair ripped pockets on good shirts we weren't supposed to wrestle in or play tackle football in. And he seemed glad to do it for us. Yep, the Frog had a passel of good common sense and life skill but never could master his multiplication tables or the cursive *D*. All in all, we needed Froggie in Post Oak, Georgia.

Chief Alston was the first to acknowledge Froggie, and it wasn't pleasant. "Get outta here, Roundbottom. Don't bother us. This is somethin' you'ins don't know nothin' about. Yore too damned dumb to even be here. Go on, now. Git. And take them other boys with you."

Sheriff Samuels was equally as courteous. "Yore in the way, boy. That ambi . . . ambix . . . ambrosias ability you got ain't helpful at all to us right now. You know your paw's about to finish up his time in jail this month, and he'll beat the crap outta you if you do anythin' to keep the two of you from goin' home. Get on. Get on back outta the way."

Only the truck driver seemed curious about Froggie's presence. By this point, you see, he was growing desperate. "What is it, boy? You got somethin' to say? You seen anythin' like this before? Speak up or get the hell back behind them there cars."

The Frog looked down . . . then up . . . then back down again. He mumbled something indistinguishable. Sheriff Samuels intervened again. "Dammit, I done told you to get back away from us. We's tryin' to figure this mess out, and you can't help us none." The discordant horn blowing and yelling from the stalled drivers had increased to pretty much fever pitch. One guy was even insisting that someone blow up the underpass. And another really big fellow unhappy with his forced stay in Post Oak was getting out of his car.

Froggie looked back up and directly at the truck driver. "I think . . . I think . . . if you'ins would let some air out of them there trailer tires, then . . . then the truck might settle a little bit and not be jammed any more. Then y'all might be able to drive 'er out. You might could try it."

I've seen a lot in life, I reckon. I've seen three car wrecks, one small plane that slid off a runway and into a cotton field, a college running back whose leg was so twisted in a tackle that everything below the right knee was headed in the wrong direction, three North Georgia goat ropings, and even the 1960 Cotton Bowl in Dallas when an integrated Syracuse team soundly whipped the deeply segregated Texas Longhorns. But I've never seen anything like the expressions on those grown men's faces after what Froggie had said took hold. I'll bet the Neanderthals who watched one of their own start the first fire—or the folks who heard Sir Isaac Newton explain gravity—or even the factory workers who listened as Henry Ford described the first assembly line—I'll bet all of these people felt as if they'd been given a blinding glimpse of the obvious. So had Chief Alston, Sheriff Samuels, the Georgia Highway Patrolman, and the beleaguered truck driver for Swift Meats. The chief finally recovered enough to have the presence of mind to grab Froggie by the shoulders and usher him back to where Weaver and I were standing. "OK, Roundbottom," Chief Alston said, "you stay back here for a while. We'll see if your silly idea works."

Well, it did. It took about thirty minutes for the tires to be deflated sufficiently to separate the trailer's top from the concrete underpass. It took another twenty minutes to direct the closest backed-up traffic far enough off the road to enable the big truck to move out of the underpass and slowly lumber on to Raeford's Service Station south of Post Oak, where the huge tires could be re-aired. I was happy to watch as the word of Froggie's genius spread back on either side of the monumental traffic jam. It was certainly something to see! As the cars slowly drove by, most of the occupants leaned out of various windows and waved at Froggie, cheered, and even applauded. The Frog had never in his life had this sort of affirmation. And he probably never would again. The last car on the north-to-south side, from Michigan, moved slowly by, and the teenage kid in the back seat gave the thumbs up to Froggie and the single finger salute to the official Post Oak delegation standing nearby. I think I saw his mother slap him as he withdrew the salute. None of us ever had the guts to render the bird to our town's officials, and we really admired the yankee kid from Michigan. Froggie just waved.

It took little time for all that commotion to die down. All of the Post Oak working folk went back to their jobs, including the Markson brothers, who argued all the way back to their barber shop. Aunt Lattie's luncheon clientele returned to their now-cold meatloaf platters. The highway patrolman got back into his car and drove north, back out of town toward the state line. Chief Alston and Mayor Reynolds talked for a few minutes then went their separate ways. I kicked back my bike's kickstand, motioned for Froggie to hop on, and joined Weaver as we bicycled over toward my house.

When we arrived home, the Frog got off and started walking across the street toward the jail. Weaver headed on to his house. I decided that something else was needed. Frog was still in earshot. "Hey, Froggie," I said, "you done a good thing back there. They'd still be tryin' to figger out how to get that truck unstuck if you hadn't said somethin'. You're OK, Frog."

"Nah, Lockhart," he replied. "They'd have figgered that 'un out sooner or later. But it shore was fun while it lasted. I really thought the sher'ff was smarter'n that. I guess not. See ya tomorrow."

As Froggie ambled on toward the jail, I noticed that Seth's arms were hanging out the bars of one of the second story windows as he motioned to his son. I heard his gruff reprimand: "Boy, what happened out there? Did you do somethin' to cause trouble? By God, you'ins knows I'll tan you good if you crossed up the sher'ff. We gotta get outta here and get home. I got customers to tend to. You get your ass back in here and settle down. You hear me!"

Froggie sort of waved and nodded at ol' Seth, turned back to me, and shrugged his shoulders. Then he walked to the "Colored Only" labeled, badly stained and precariously hanging water fountain outside the jail's back door, took a long sip of the tepid water, and went on in to the jail's first floor and to his flour sacks in the storage closet. This was Froggie's way of saying "up yours" to a system of separate government that didn't assist Roundbottoms or the abject poor of any race. The Frog's gesture was futile but admirable, in a hopeless kind of way.

I'd watched our friend do this many times before. This small protest always seemed to perk our friend up as he disappeared into the jail. He needed something like this, probably. Yep, all things considered, the Frog was OK.

Miss Fancy Drives to Town

I've said it before, but despite its obvious truth, it bears repeating. Small towns anywhere in the South have their special characters. Some of these folks come by it naturally: they were born defective in a tiny way or two, having come from a family line that didn't succeed genetically; or, as one of our town's down-to-earth businessmen used to say, "That ol' boy (or gal) just ain't rite in the haid." I guess there are other places where a person "ain't rite," but the "haid" has to be close to the top. Sorry. For instance, one of Post Oak's noteworthy specials, Up and Down, walked each day the full length of the town— maybe a mile—turned around and reversed his tracks back to the starting point. Back and forth. Up and down. Continually. Every day. He couldn't help it.

Some other of these citizens strived within themselves for this unique character status: they played practical jokes, they lollygagged around on street corners to panhandle or to start up never ending conversations, or occasionally they broke into the local hardware store or diner or grammar school to steal something and found themselves in trouble and consigned for a month to the county work farm. I guess we all do what we're compelled to do.

Still other characters became such because they lived on the complete opposite side of any of this stuff I've just mentioned and stood out accordingly and even obsessively. These were the good ones—too good, usually—who went to church when the doors were cracked only slightly, paid their bills on time, delivered clothes and turkeys to the poor at Thanksgiving, attended local civic group meetings, acquired reputations for pristine conduct, maybe even taught school. Thus, we had Miss Fancy Emmons, a character of eloquence, of deep Methodist faith, of substantial education, of deep gray and bunned-up hair, of tidy if decades in arrears fashion, and of celebrated spinsterhood. On this, her particular day in the spotlight, she also proudly sported a newly issued Georgia driver's license. Miss Fancy had never had a driver's license, and she was almost seventy-five years old. It can only get better from here.

Miss Fancy was the English teacher with the most seniority at Post Oak High School, my alma mater. She taught me during the 1964-1965 academic year when I was in the 11th grade, and she had taught my mother when Mom was in the 11th grade. This was as far as you could go when Mom went to school; but in 1965 I still had my twelfth-grade year to go. Lord knows, I needed it!

Miss Fancy had taught most of the moms and dads of most of the guys and gals I knew in school. And Miss Fancy and my grandmother were the best of friends until Granny died in 1958. Miss Fancy was beyond mandatory retirement age, but no one was counting, and her older brother, Mr. Tom Emmons, was our school's assistant principal who, many years earlier, had served as the county school superintendent. By the way, *nepotism* was a word no one knew much about or cared much about in Post Oak, Georgia, in 1965. Miss Fancy, her brother, and her brother's wife lived on a well-tended farm about six miles south of Post Oak.

Miss Fancy's personality was a little quirky for the time. She was a formidable woman, straight-laced and overly precise about everything. She enunciated articulately, a contradiction for a north Georgian living among those who usually talked like the lead family in the short-lived TV series set near Macon, *Here Comes Honey Boo-Boo*. She made proper distinctions between *lie* and *lay* and between *sit* and *set*. Her verbs always agreed with their subjects, and her pronouns always agreed with their antecedents. She knew how to use a semicolon in writing. Imagine that! She didn't hesitate to correct those who would speak egregiously in her presence; the size of the audience didn't matter. She seemed to relish her corrective sessions with our Methodist preacher after church, going after him especially if he misused in his sermon the case of the pronouns *she/her* or *he/him* in prepositional phrases. One Sunday she reamed him rather well because his vague pronoun reference obscured the specific identities in context of the prodigal son and his older brother in the famous parable. Overhearing this sharply honed criticism of the preacher one Sunday, I wondered whether God was pleased with these pontificating directives or whether even English teachers could step too far. But, you know, I imagine Miss Fancy has had time by now to assign grammar and usage exercises to God for His elucidation as He awaits the next international crisis.

The world according to Miss Fancy Emmons was a rigid, austere, grim, serious world and one which was molded by her to fit her own vision. I knew this to be true. I experienced it. I lived a personal vignette that placed me smack dab in the middle of this world.

In her English teacher status, this lady had always assumed the role of director of most of the senior plays that were performed at Post Oak High School. As somehow fitting, *Arsenic and Old Lace* was selected in the spring of 1966 to be our senior play. Because I had acted in a few dramatic productions previously and had not, I don't think, stepped on myself too badly on stage, Miss Fancy decided that I would do nicely for the role of the slightly deranged fellow who thinks he's Teddy Roosevelt. Remember? She cornered me one day outside the school store to unquestionably voice her expectation that I would appear in the play. You were always a little scared to be cornered by Miss Emmons. The reason for the cornering was never in your favor. I thanked her but politely responded that I played baseball and that my practices and games after school would conflict with play rehearsals. Either she didn't hear me or didn't care. "Michael Lockhart," she slowly began, piercing me with her steel gray eyes. "Michael, you must be in this play. I've decided it. You are needed. Your silly baseball games aren't nearly as important as the senior play. Your mother would want this. And your grandmother, God rest her sweet soul, would be so disappointed in you for not being with us."

"But Miss Emmons," I replied, "I've played baseball all my life. I love baseball. We finally have a decent team that might win region and get to go to Atlanta this year. This means a lot to me. Please . . . do you understand?"

She didn't.

I extricated myself awkwardly but respectfully.

Just before ball practice started after school the next day, I realized that I had left my history textbook in my locker, and we would have a test the following day. Before Coach Jenkins called us together and before the custodian locked the outer side door nearest my locker, I jogged back into the school. I was in my practice uniform, and my spikes were noisy on the concrete floor as I moved quickly to the first row of senior lockers. Somehow, I didn't see her. She must have seen me walk in and waited in ambush. In the next instant this small but gritty woman had seized my left arm and bounced me up against the light green cinder block wall. She was adamant: "Michael, what are you doing in this ridiculous outfit and wearing these dangerous shoes? Rehearsals begin in 45 minutes. Be there."

I tried twice more to explain my decision to stay with baseball, moving a tad bit forward and toward the side door with each plea. Both times she bounced me back against the wall. "Your mother was an outstanding thespian, and I never had to convince her of her proper duties at school. You are about to betray your fine family name, young man." We all knew that Miss Emmons had long fought a before-its-time fight to limit helmets, shoulder pads, jock straps, and baseball bats for the sake of better stage facilities and pay for music and art teachers at dear old Post Oak High. Heck, she might have been the only person around Post Oak to have even seen a live Broadway play! Maybe in this confrontation I represented all that was trashy about dreaded redneck sports as compared to the aesthetic beauty of drama and, indeed, all of art. I don't know. But I did know that if I couldn't extract myself from this awkward conversation soon, I'd be late to practice and would incur the opportunity to run the perimeter of our ball field four or five times before infield drills ended.

Desperate to exit my encounter with this determined and frustrated old woman, I blurted out too forcefully, "Miss Emmons, I don't want to be in this silly play! I don't want to spend all of my free time rehearsing! I don't want to be a crazy Teddy Roosevelt! Don't you understand? I want to play baseball. Please don't fuss at me! Now please excuse me."

As I brushed past her toward the door and stepped out into the walkway beyond, I quickly looked back. I think I expected to see smoke coming from her angry red face and ears and perhaps runs of slobber at the corners of her mouth. This old biddy was messing with my true love of baseball and my last year of playing the sport. I had neither the hand-eye coordination nor the pure skill to catch up to a college-level fastball or to hit a good outside curve, so I had little time left to relish my true love. All of this flittered past my mind as I glanced back into the school. But Miss Emmons seemed not to be uncontrollably mad. She just stood in place, having been refused by a student for probably one of the few times in her teaching life. She looked directly back at me. Our eyes met. She turned, bowed her head, and ambled unevenly back down the hall. She was disappointed . . . and hurt. And I was the cause. While the skills of tact and diplomacy usually shielded me from some bad fist fights, these talents escaped me in a conflict with an iconic old English teacher.

But the focus here is on Miss Fancy Emmons' driving career. It's necessary to know that Miss Fancy had been contemplating a driving life phase for some time. She knew that many in Post Oak whispered around that her old maidishness was never better symbolized than by her inability—or unwillingness—to drive a car. She was also weary of her dependence on her brother and his deep brown 1962 Ford Fairlane for her basic transportation to work, to town for errands, and even to Chattanooga, the large city just across the state line, for necessary shopping trips. Quietly and surreptitiously, she arranged for her sister-in-law, Nelle, to provide the driving lessons. This plan worked imperfectly, at best. Miss Fancy practiced mainly around the farm, and, miraculously enough, only two fence posts, one rusty furrow plow, and one slow old laying hen became the only casualties. After the third testing attempt, Miss Fancy was issued the treasured State of Georgia driver's license, no strings attached.

Fast forward a few weeks. It was a clear, windy, coolish day in late October. Markson's Barber Shop, a small but visible business in a neat row of six or seven brick businesses, sat almost directly across Cleburne Street from the Bank of Post Oak. Our bank was the most regal and tallest building in town, an imposing, three-story, slightly classical architectural accomplishment constructed in 1939 when the ruinous Depression was easing up and Post Oak folks were getting over their tendency to secure their meager savings under mattresses. The bank was always the first thing viewed when the barber shop clients looked out the large window to scan the happenings on Cleburne Street.

The characters frequenting the barbershop on this fairly normal day were, at the least, interesting. There were the barbers, of course. Joe and Wellman Markson, brothers although not especially close associates with practically no usual blood regard for each other, waxed eloquent with their (often conflicting) views on the upcoming county commissioner election, the desirability of keeping Herman Talmadge as our state's junior senator, the delayed opening of the long-promised welcome center off I-75 just north of town, and Coach Bradley's continuing habit of investing our mediocre high school football team with his mediocre playbook of "run right, run left, run up the middle, punt."

I was waiting in the shop for my turn in a chair, along with my best buddy, Will Weaver. Three other guys occupied seat-ripped chairs salvaged from a well-used, red Formica dining table suite. Old Tater Patterson, a hog raiser from the Rising Buck community over in the east valley, was in Joe's chair, with two droplets of tobacco juice—one new and the other a bit used—sliding into his disheveled whiskers and with one top button of his overalls hanging askew over the once white barber's smock. Tater sure was a class act. The other boys from Rising Buck didn't make it to town often. This was a good thing. You see, Tater was kind of the self-appointed head of a large group of brothers, cousins, delinquent (but the term wasn't used then) kids, "rode hard and put up wet" women, and one weathered old granny who might or might not have been their kin, all of whom lived together in two, pieced-together, ramshackle cabins next to a wet-weather creek. Tater felt an obligation to get a quarterly haircut, even if he didn't need one. Usually, Joe insisted on giving Tater a shampoo before the cutting could begin, but let's not dwell on this.

161

Last but certainly not least and sitting somewhat royally in Wellman's chair was John Quinn, the incumbent county commissioner. John was overweight and always wore dingy white dress shirts with neck sizes long since outgrown that allowed partially tied and wrinkled neckties to reveal unbuttoned and gapping shirt collars. He was prone to self-glorifying assurances about his strong work ethic and remained always mindful of his need to garner votes.

To John's credit, he had supported his mother and three siblings after his dad ran off during the boy's first year of high school. With lacking academic prowess, he had barely scraped by in high school around thirty years earlier. Somehow, it was told, he had managed to talk himself out of an alleged cheating incident regarding one of Miss Fancy's poetry tests. He had been caught dead to rights. No one ever emerged unscathed from this kind of problem with Miss Fancy Emmons, but John did. Those Post Oak natives around at the time rumored that she actually felt sorry for him, a trait of sympathy not often demonstrated by this harsh, usually unforgiving woman. Whatever the case, John was always helpful and respectful to Miss Fancy following his close call with expulsion.

Yep, ol' John held court proudly in Wellman's chair on this crisp October day. He was telling jokes and seeking votes and letting all within earshot know that he was an important guy. Indeed, our county commissioner was one of the few gentlemen in Post Oak who added a one-dollar shave to his normal haircut, and by this time he was fully lathered and awaiting the cool feel of Wellman's just stropped razor. Then it happened.

Miss Fancy came up Cleburne Street in her brother's Fairlane, stopped abruptly in front of the bank, and pulled diagonally—well, sort of—into a vacant parking space. On one side was Jimbo Felker's yellow DeSoto; on Miss Fancy's driver's side was John Quinn's new Ford F-100 pickup. You have to know that John loved this truck almost as much as he loved his

162

bourbon and foxhounds and a little tiny bit more than he loved his wife. We watched with idle interest as Miss Fancy opened her driver's side door, maneuvered out from under the steering wheel, and stepped determinedly to the sidewalk. She paused momentarily and peered into the cabin of the F-100, more out of annoyance than admiration, I'm sure. Then she walked into the bank. Will leaned over and whispered, "Watch when she comes out. This'll be really good." Will's aunt and uncle lived near the Emmons farm, and Will had spied on Miss Fancy during the driving lesson fun. Will knew exactly what to expect.

Her bank business didn't take long. In fact, John's shave wasn't even over by the time she came out, and he, too—along with most of the rest of us—was casually glancing across the street. Miss Fancy opened her car door and repositioned herself behind the steering wheel. Realizing that Cleburne Street— or 41 highway, as it was better known—carried a good bit of traffic, she cautiously put the car into "R," peered into the rear-view mirror, and began her emergence. However, her aim was off—or her inexperience took over—or the sun was too much in her eyes—because the brown Fairlane jerked to its left and scraped John's F-100 in a nasty, sliding, three-foot gash across the right rear fender well. Bright red and deep brown paint coalesced to become a sour looking, rusty color on the back part of the pickup. We could see her react with a quick head turn. Not to be outdone, Miss Fancy shifted into "D" and pulled toward the sidewalk. She probably thought the damage was minimal. She backed again, and this time—Bam!—the Fairlane removed a chrome strip and the side F-100 insignia, all of which fell awkwardly to the pavement and sort of bounced under the truck. Forward she went again to the curb in an effort to straighten her steering wheel.

By this second collision, Will and I—and the rest of the Marksons' clientele—had moved slowly toward the large front window which afforded a panoramic view of Cleburne Street and the bank. Will whispered, "God-a-mighty! Boy, ain't this good! I knew she couldn't get outta there clean!" Then it was that John Quinn sprinted past us with a squeaky grunt and a loping gait toward the front door of the barbershop. His smock still attached and his face still partly lathered white but red underneath, John struggled to get to his new pickup in time to save it. The shop door didn't open for John on his first pull, so he hissed "Dammit!" and yanked back with enough force to loosen the knob and shake the door's shade almost out of its brackets. "Boy, he's pissed," Will shared to no one in particular. John bounded from the barber shop and might have made it to the street in time to stop further damage—except for Freddy Gandy's Radio Flyer wagon parked in front of the shop door. The wagon was full of empty Coke, Pepsi, and RC bottles Freddy was pulling to the local Shop-Rite for the deposit money. John stumbled into the wagon, tried to step over it, lost his balance, and fell forward into an unused parking space. He reached out with both hands to brace his fall, and this plan generally worked. He didn't really hurt himself, but on its way down, his right hand grazed a softening plug of Tater's Red Man chewing tobacco spat down in the space as Tater had entered the barbershop thirty minutes earlier. As John righted himself and continued running across the street, he wiped his hand on his slacks then up along the right side of his face then across his forehead. Most, but not all, of Tater's prime plug and lather were left on the slacks. A small line of brown residue ran in a squiggly smudge from above John's left eye to his receding hairline, and this irregular smudge was accented by occasional flecks of the now-stained shaving cream. This effect was rather unusual, even for Post Oak, Georgia.

By this time, Miss Fancy had backed almost completely into the street—almost. As she turned the wheel to complete her most recent backing maneuver, the left front bumper of the Fairlane caught the right rear bumper of the truck, partly dislodging this heretofore unscathed part of the pickup. The pickup's rear bumper hung limply, bent and scratched. John raced to the driver's side of the Fairlane and implored Miss Fancy to stop. She did.

As Miss Fancy rolled down her driver's side window, John began to survey the damage. "Doggone it, Miss Emmons," he started. "You've done messed up my new truck, and I was a-gonna drive this truck in the homecomin' parade tomorrow. Doggone it! I've already ordered my campaign posters and everthin' for both doors of the truck. Doggone it!" The "Doggone it!" was much less severe than what ol' John wanted to say in keeping with the situation.

"Don't take on so, John," Miss Fancy replied, assuming her experienced teacher, in-control posture from her many years in the classroom. "I didn't mean to hit your truck. I'll arrange to have it fixed. Now I must move along and not block this heavy traffic any longer."

John's exasperation cooled. He must have decided that his new red Ford pick-up wasn't worth an attempted chewing out and embarrassment of a respected old lady who had once done him a very good turn. Besides, he might look bad in front of a small crowd of Post Oak voters. And besides that, he might lose the verbal confrontation. You could see his shoulders sort of slouch as he responded, "Yes, ma'am. Let me stop these here cars so you can back out safely." He moved into the busy street—smock, facial tobacco stains, and all—and held up the two lines of vehicles while the brown Fairlane completed its backing, straightened out, and slowly moved south away from the horrific scene. He also shook his head in the direction of Officer Frank Frazier, one of Post Oak's two policemen, who had rushed toward the Fairlane with ticket book drawn. "It's OK, Frank," said John. "I'll take care of it with Miss Emmons." John must have figured that his influence in Post Oak would preclude the need for a written police report submitted to the insurance company. Heck, I'll bet the local Georgia Farm Bureau insurance agent wouldn't have welcomed a meeting with Miss Fancy either.

John lovingly touched the wounds in his truck's fender and jaywalked on across the street back toward the barbershop. Slowly, he shook his head and used the smock to dab at the rapidly hardening mess on his face. We watched as he trudged back in, resumed his place in Wellman's chair, and leaned his head back for his shave to continue. No one said anything. There was pretty much nothing to say.

Squib

F orrest Gump was totally on the mark, you know: "Life *is* often like a box of chocolates; you never know what you're going to get" (italics mine). One wonderful day at my teenage place of employment, a large supermarket called the Red Food Store, my dad and I were privy to an event that became legendary in the annals of grocery business history in North Georgia.

Let me not go too much farther without saying that this story might not be suitable for young readers and somewhat older Southern ladies. But I don't consider myself a chauvinist, and censorship isn't something I promote. What the heck, drive on!

My first regular paying job—other than mowing yards, ordering greeting cards from an ad on the back of a *Rin Tin Tin* comic book and unsuccessfully trying to sell them, slopping my cousin's hogs, or cleaning out local barns—was the combined position of stock clerk and bag boy in a supermarket. This was maybe late 1964. My dad was a meat cutter at this store and had arranged for me to work there when I turned sixteen. The job paid a largess of $1.15/hour, and I was expected to work after school on Fridays from 3:30 – 10:30 p.m. and all day on Saturday. Do I ever recall the excitement of landing the job and telling my buddies all about it! Having reached the pivotal age of sixteen, a milestone that brought a source of income as well as the longed-for, unrestricted Georgia driver's license,

I was certain that the way was now clear for the unbounded pursuit of women. Yeah! My ability to reason into the future was still quite limited, however, and it hadn't occurred to me that a weekend job might provide a tad of money and a driving benefit but would interfere with the vital free Friday and Saturday evening times so necessary for these searches in the first place. Alas. It's obvious that this limited reasoning skill indicates my maturity of thought at the time.

The subject of this story—Squib, my co-worker—was a tall, balding fellow near thirty years of age. Squib's tragic flaw, if such could be assumed, was his condition of epilepsy. This unfortunate disease caused him to pass out occasionally with unpredictable seizures. The poor fellow would strike a transfixed stare, become rigid, weave side to side, then fall to the floor. He would remain comatose for several minutes until one of our older supervisors would assist him to recover. When he came to, he never seemed to realize what had just happened.

The first time I observed one of Squib's seizures, when he fell against me as we stood near the time clock in the storeroom, I was really scared. That day I eased Squib to the floor in a panicky sort of way. Over time, I got used to the poor guy's condition, I guess. Today, in the third decade of the 21st century, either more effective treatment plans exist for this malady or the victim would live in a facility designed to mitigate the effects of the disease. But in 1964, in Cranwell, Georgia, a larger neighboring community between my home town of Post Oak and Chattanooga, assistance for epilepsy was not very sophisticated and probably more expensive than Squib's folks could handle. Our store manager, Roy Dickert, not necessarily a paragon of compassion, somehow felt sorry for Squib and gave him work. Mr. Dickert was also willing to overlook Squib's propensity for immature behavior probably related to the poor guy's condition but not always in keeping with Squib's advanced age of thirty. This behavior often took the form of sharing dirty jokes and foul language with my other work buddies and me as well as sniffing out any opportunity for a practical joke.

On the day of this fascinating event, I had clocked in at 3:25 p.m., tied on my apron, and proceeded to the store's checkout area to begin my usual job of moving behind one of the six cashiers, bagging groceries, loading the sacks (paper—plastic bags were unheard of then) into a cart, and dutifully following the customer to her or his car. With due regard for modesty, I was pretty good at this process, a pleasant talker, and usually finished my shift with a pocketful of tip change. I never mis-bagged eggs or squished bread, for example. Let's choose not to focus on the day I scraped my cart along the door and right fender of a dapper customer's recently refurbished 1957 T-Bird.

This time, after my first carry-out, the assistant manager told me to go to the back storeroom and bring up three or four cases of new bags. I didn't mind this order because it gave me a chance to watch one of the brand new and even more naïve than I bagboys search desperately for "paper bag stretchers." Think about that. And turnover among bag boys was substantial, so we always had two or three rookies reporting for duty each week. Squib really enjoyed taking part in this prank, but on this day it was David McNeal who sent the neophyte running to the storeroom, dodging customers, and flailing about in an all-out, life-or-death quest for these stretchers. Usually, my dad or an older and kinder stock clerk would calm the young fellow down, pat him gently on the shoulder, and explain the rather ridiculous concept of a "bag stretcher." Then the newbie would walk dejectedly and embarrassingly back to his post in the front of the store. As a bagboy newcomer to the Red Food Store supermarket culture, you were required to go through this rite of passage. (I did, and you can see how this initiation experience prepared me effectively for life.) But on this remarkable day in question, I wasn't able to watch the bag stretcher fun. Not by a long shot. There was bigger fun.

My trek to the back of the store for the new bags ended around thirty feet from the left side of our large meat case. I stopped abruptly to notice in front of me a distinguished lady, Mrs. Parkman, chatting with my dad about a particular roast she needed for her next Sunday dinner. She was on the front side of the meat counter; my dad was across from her near the door to the butchering and cooler area. I watched as she pointed to the large piece of meat and explained precisely how she wanted Dad to handle the additional trimming. He listened intently and politely, not wishing to bring his thirty plus years of unionized Journeyman Meat Cutter experience to bear on this opinionated lady. Mrs. Parkman was familiar to me since I had bagged and carried out her groceries many times. She was a fair tipper. I knew that she lived in one of the larger homes on Missionary Ridge, in fact, in one of the "rich folks'" homes. She was very nice, quite prim and proper, a tad portly, and always dressed to the nines. On this day she wore a light green skirt, wide belt, matching blouse, colorful scarf, and more fancy jewelry than necessary for a routine grocery shopping trip. At times, Mrs. Parkman could be a bit pretentious.

Out of the corner of my eye and right before I started to speak to her, I noticed Squib approaching the meat case pushing one grocery cart and pulling another, full, as they were, of empty Coke, Pepsi, Mountain Dew, and RC bottles returned to the store for deposit. The management of these empty deposit bottles was Squib's main job at the Red Food Store. He performed it well. Squib nodded to me, winked, then paused in his walk to the bottle storage area. I should have picked up on the sly warning, but I couldn't for the life of me figure out Squib's intent. I could see that he was noticing Mrs. Parkman and her conversation with Dad. By now, she had pointed to another roast farther from her and was leaning way over the counter, almost to the point of leaving her high heels for a better view and explanation. She was close to a complete prone position across the counter, not ladylike but necessary to her decision about the Sunday roast. What happened next was a precious gift to me, an awkward as hell moment for my dad, and a story that lived for years and was still told by store retirees at the time of the Red Food Store's merger with Bi-Lo.

Whether Squib was moving toward one of his seizures or whether he recognized an opportunity for some real fun, he "seized the day" most opportunely. He left the two carts and walked quickly but unobtrusively toward Mrs. Parkman. Now my dad always blamed me for not intervening in what happened next, but I'll swear on a stack of King James Bibles that I couldn't have predicted the impending glory.

Mrs. Parkman had by this time relaxed her most extensive stretch to the elusive roast and was beginning to conclude her business with Dad. Even so, she was still bent way over the meat case with one hand bracing on a rack divider. She hadn't yet seen Squib. The roast selection—and Dad's assent regarding this fine lady's preparation decisions for Sunday dinner—occupied her full attention. At that moment Squib extended his right hand toward Mrs. Parkman's rather copious *derriere*, a hand now in a locked, military-style, hand salute. But instead of sharply snapping his hand to the salute position at an angle over his right eyebrow, he ran his hand gently through Mrs. Parkman's skirt and into the cleft of her buttocks while, at the same time, saying, "Check your oil, ma'am? Oops! 'Bout a quart low." Layers of undergarments and her thick dress fabric somewhat mitigated the oil check, but Mrs. Parkman had indeed felt the intervention.

It's a good bet that no one in her sheltered, refined life had ever checked Mrs. Parkman's oil in quite that vulgar a manner. Two reactions happened at once: she let forth with a pronounced and measured "Eek, eek!" scream while leaping forward across the meat counter with her arms outstretched toward Dad. She had left the floor entirely, had lost one of her high heels, and was lying fully extended over the packaged rib eyes and a row of sirloin tips. Squib calmly went back to his carts and began to roll them toward the storeroom, whistling *O, Susanna* as he walked. Since it was a Saturday, the store was crowded, and a good many startled customers had watched and heard the results of Squib's modified lube job.

Dad braced Mrs. Parkman from his side of the meat case. I began to help her wiggle and inch back toward the floor, assisted by Ronnie Hopkins, a bagger who had also witnessed the entire affair, and another female customer who happened to be Mrs. Parkman's next-door neighbor, Nellie Tharpe. This coincidence couldn't be good. When the disarrayed and flustered lady had at last shaken off our efforts at assistance and righted herself, she pierced my dad with a penetrating stare and demanded to see the manager "right now." I rushed to the manager's office near the store's front door, got Mr. Dickert's attention, and breathlessly uttered, "Mr. Dickert, you gotta come back to the meat department right now. Squib just checked Mrs. Parkman's oil, and she didn't want her oil checked. Please come now!"

"What do you mean?" Dickert replied. When I mimicked the hand-up-the-butt action, he cried, "Oh, my God! Is the lady hurt? What's she saying? Where's Squib?" He put forth these questions while we both quickly retraced my path down the condiments aisle. I had only partially answered his first question by the time we reached the scene of the action. Dickert reached out to the rapidly reddening lady and took her solicitously by the right arm. He began, "Mrs. Parkman, are you hurt? I can't begin . . ."

That's as far as he got. She forcefully brushed off Dickert's consoling touch as if he were infested with some incurable disease and began a tirade laced with expressions not entirely appropriate for a well-bred Southern lady. "Wicked pervert," "damned low-life heathen," and "worthless son-of-a-bitch" were the milder outpourings enunciated before she realized her neighbor, Nellie Tharpe, was at the scene and in earshot. Mrs. Parkman calmed down a bit, jerked her high-heeled shoe from my hand, and limped toward the front of the store without replacing the shoe. Her off-stepping gait was made more fascinating by the pulling up and sticking of the back left side of her skirt and slip to her wide belt, a fashion design that exposed a section of panties and upper thigh. These clothing rearrangements had happened during her leap over the meat counter and while Ronnie and I tried to pull her back to safe ground. Nellie rushed to Mrs. Parkman and adroitly adjusted the riding up skirt and under garments, a feat made more difficult by Mrs. Parkman's refusal to slow her pace. Roy Dickert sort of trotted beside her, apologizing and explaining in equal measure: "Mrs. Parkman, I'm so very sorry this has happened. Our employee's behavior in no way represents the quality of food and service you've come to expect from our Red Food Store. I intend to dismiss . . ."

He was not able to finish. Mrs. Parkman, by this time, had reached the front door and somehow had replaced her missing shoe in stride. She paused long enough to fire a parting shot: "Mr. Dickert, no words can express my anger and embarrassment at this moment. My husband will know about this within the hour. And before closing time this evening, our attorney will contact you regarding the civil damages and criminal behavior committed. I'm sure your store will want to do the right thing. In fact, I'm damned sure of it!"

Believe it or not, after the smoke cleared from this spectacle, the anticipated court action and personnel dismissal didn't happen. Well, not entirely. When Mrs. Parkman discovered that Squib suffered from epilepsy and bouts of erratic behavior and that Mr. Dickert had given him work for a number of years, the high-toned lady found compassion herself and dropped the issue. Nellie shared with Dad a few weeks later that Mrs. Parkman's husband had motivated some of his wife's compassion but only after he could discuss the event without laughing. Coping with a stressful and somewhat embarrassing situation can normally be helped along with a good sense of humor. And Dickert fired Squib—temporarily—but brought him back to the bottle deposit job in three weeks or so. It hadn't been and wasn't to be the only firing and re-hiring procedure for Squib.

I left the Red Food Store job two years following the oil check episode. During my senior year of college, I read Squib's obituary in the *Chattanooga Times* and learned from Dad that one of the poor fellow's seizures had caused him to fall down a flight of stairs at a local department store. The fall was fatal. Mrs. Parkman, her dignity long since intact, had decided to continue to shop at the store and to ask for my dad to help her select and trim out choice cuts of beef. This was good. She and her husband made a substantial memorial gift to a local hospital in Squib's honor after they learned of his death. This was also good.

Forrest's chocolates can almost always be an apt metaphor for life. Don't smirk. You know it's the truth.

About the Author

Over his 37-year career, Michael Broome, Professor Emeritus of English, served as head of the division of languages and literatures, associate dean of the college, and dean of the graduate school and academic services at Columbia College, Columbia, South Carolina. He is a retired lieutenant colonel with the South Carolina Army National Guard. He holds a B.A. from the University of Chattanooga, an M.A. from Florida State University, and a Ph.D. from the University of South Carolina. He points to his mom and to his mentor at the University of Chattanooga, Professor George Connor, as his inspirations to "keep writing." He and his wife, Charlotte, a retired associate dean of evening college admissions at Columbia College, enjoy travel with a special group of friends in Columbia and leisure time at family homes at Pawley's Island, South Carolina, and Maggie Valley, North Carolina. Michael's hobbies include reading, gardening, Civil War and World War II history, and baseball card collecting.

Both Michael and his wife remain as active as possible in their beloved and historical Washington Street United Methodist Church in Columbia, South Carolina.